Dear Scott,

It's been a pleasure working with you the last several years. We hope you enjoy the book!

Alena Reinhfer
and

Julius Reinitzer

2012

The Nine Lives of Julius

The Nine Lives of Julius

A True Story of Survival

Ilona Reinitzer

To order additional copies of this book, contact:
Xlibris Corporation
1-888-795-4274
www.Xlibris.com
Orders@Xlibris.com
119197

DEDICATION

This book is dedicated to all the soldiers in the armed forces (past, present, and future) for their dedication in fighting for our freedom.

CHAPTER 1

I T WAS A warm and sunny day in June 1938 when my brothers and I were planning our annual camping trip. Each summer, Jiri, my older brother, Jan, my twin, and I would head south of Prague and camp along the Moldau, Berounka, and Sazava Rivers. We would meet many of our friends there and spend the days swimming and hiking.

Each evening around the campfire, we would tell stories about things we had read in magazines about the United States. We loved telling stories about cowboys and tried to imitate everything we had read about them. We cooked our breakfast over the campfire and made bacon, eggs, and beans because that was what cowboys ate. We also talked about Hollywood, Broadway, Wall Street, the Statue of Liberty, and anything else we could think of that we had read. It was my dream to visit this great country that had so much glamor and excitement. I was ten years old at the time, and life in Czechoslovakia was fun and carefree.

Life in the past wasn't always that carefree, and little did I know what the future years would have in store for me. My parents, Jan and Jirina, had told me stories about how bad things were during World War I and during the Depression of 1929; however, in 1931, the Czechoslovakian economy started to improve, and by 1938, Prague was one of the most prosperous countries in Europe. My family was doing well, and, therefore, my brothers and I were given lessons in music and foreign languages. My father always insisted that we learn to speak German since that was the language of our neighboring countries. In our spare time, my brother and I loved to play soccer, so we always tried to organize a game with the other kids in the neighborhood whenever we found time.

One day, we were returning home from a soccer game when we ran into some older boys fishing on the banks of the Moldau. I recognized them from the soccer field where they had played earlier.

"Hey, kiddies, what are you doing so far away from your mommies?" one of the boys asked.

"None of your damn business," I replied. I wasn't about to let these older boys intimidate me.

"Look, guys, one of them thinks he's a tough guy," the biggest boy said.

"Yeah, well, I'm certainly a lot tougher than any of you," I said.

"Come on, Julius, let's just go home," Jan begged.

"Oh yeah, what makes you so tough?" one of the other boys asked.

"I can do anything you can do," I answered.

"How about jumping off the bridge?" the biggest boy asked.

"I will do it if you do it with me," I replied.

"Let's go then," he said.

"Are you crazy?" Jan asked.

"It's no big deal. I'm not scared," I answered him. I was always the feistiest of my brothers, and my big mouth was always getting me into some kind of trouble.

ILONA REINITZER

"That bridge is way too high up. You are going to kill yourself!" Jan exclaimed.

We all headed over to the middle of the bridge, and the biggest boy and I stood on the edge of the bridge.

"So are we jumping in or diving in?" I asked.

The boy looked down at the water and all of a sudden became very nervous. He was realizing just how far down the water was.

"I'm not jumping in. For all I know, you will chicken out once I jump," he said.

"Well, I could say the same for you, so I guess this means you are the chicken," I replied.

"You weren't really going to jump. You were just saying it to be tough," he said.

"I will bet you your soccer ball that I will jump," I said.

"Go for it. He will never do it," one of his friends said to him.

"All right, but you have to dive off head first if you want the soccer ball," he agreed.

My brothers and I had to share one soccer ball, and so I really wanted a ball of my own. I was also dying to take his soccer ball from him, so I agreed to dive in headfirst.

I looked down and the water was dark, and I couldn't see anything below it. I had no idea how deep it was in the area that I was jumping into, but it was too late to check that out now. I took a deep breath of air and dove off the bridge. I hit the water; but then, almost immediately, my head hit the muddy river bottom. I was stuck from the shoulders down and couldn't get my head free. I thrashed about trying to free myself, and it didn't help that the water was freezing. It seemed like hours went by before I finally managed to free myself and swim up to get air. Jan told me I was actually under water for about four minutes. It was a miracle that I didn't drown or break my neck.

I did get my own soccer ball that afternoon, but I never jumped off a bridge again without knowing how deep the water was. Of course, I bragged the entire way home about how tough I was and how I had shown those older boys. I only told Jan after we got home that I thought for sure I was going to drown after I landed in the mud. From that day on, Jan would always joke that I had used up one of my "nine" lives. Little did we know that I would use up quite a few more in the next few years.

CHAPTER 2

DURING THIS TIME in Germany, Hitler was beginning to gain power and to invade neighboring countries. He took over Austria in 1938, and when the French and British economies failed, he took over the southern part of Czechoslovakia. By the end of 1939, the entire country of Czechoslovakia was occupied by the German army. In 1940, Hitler took over Poland, causing the start of World War II.

Things were drastically changing in the once peaceful and beautiful city of Prague. The Czech universities were forced to close causing demonstrations by students and the Czech underground. Jewish friends of my family were being persecuted and forced to wear the Star of David. They were not allowed to use public transportation, and eventually, they were sent to concentration camps.

One of the major events that destroyed life for Czech citizens was the massacre that took place in Lidice. In May 1942, the British army sent two Czech resistance fighters (Sergeant Jan Kubiš and Sergeant Josef Gabčík) to assassinate Reinhardt Heydrich (who was the deputy Reichsprotektor of the Nazi German Protectorate of Bohemia and Moravia). These men parachuted into Bohemia in December 1941 as part of Operation Anthropoid after being trained by the British army. On May 27, 1942, Heydrich was being driven from his country villa to his office at the Prague castle. When his car arrived at the Holešovice area of Prague, Gabčík fired a Sten gun (a British 9 mm submachine gun) at Heydrich's car, but the gun failed to fire, so Kubiš threw a bomb at his car, which did explode. Somehow both men managed to escape the scene of the assassination. Heydrich did not die immediately from his wounds, but after surviving only a few more weeks, he died on June 4 in the Bulovka hospital in Prague from septicemia caused by pieces of upholstery entering his body when the bomb exploded.

In order to avenge Heydrich's death, the Germans waged a horrific retaliation campaign that targeted the entire Czech population including innocent civilians. The Germans chose the Czech town of Lidice because the residents here were known for their hostility toward the German occupation and because they were supposedly harboring the assassins of Heydrich. All the buildings were destroyed with explosives and then leveled until nothing remained. All the surviving men and boys over the age of sixteen (approximately, one hundred and seventy-two men and boys) were executed, and the women were sent to Ravensbrück concentration camp, where most died. Approximately, ninety children were taken to Gneisenau concentration camp, and some of them were later taken to Nazi orphanages if they were German looking.

The Gestapo then hunted down and murdered Czech citizens, resistance members, and anyone suspected of being involved in Heydrich's death, totaling over a thousand persons.

As further reprisal, three thousand Jews were deported from the ghetto at Theresienstadt for extermination. In Berlin, five hundred Jews were arrested and one hundred and fifty-two were executed.

Czech citizens were now living in terror at the hand of Nazi Germany and things were getting worse every day. The days when we had plenty of money were gone, and now there were food shortages. My family had to ration our portions, and I was constantly hungry. I was always trying to come up with ways to get more food. At dinner time, Jiri and I would convince Jan to play the game of "Emperor, King, and Beggar," where the last one to finish eating would be the beggar. This made him want to give us some of his food so he could finish first. Jiri and I only got away with that only for so long until my parents found out.

One day, my mother had put rat poison on some stale bread in the basement to kill off rodents who were trying to find food that we stored there. I found the bread while I was getting some supplies for my mother and ate it without knowing there was rat poison on it. I was just so hungry and thought she dropped some bread on the ground by accident. Amazingly, I did not get sick! My mother almost had a heart attack when she heard that I ate the rat poison. I had to admit that my brothers and I were constantly getting into some kind of trouble.

My father passed away on Christmas day of the same year leaving me and my brothers in charge of helping my mother. He died from lung cancer even though he had never smoked a day in his life. The carcinogenic chemicals from the printing press where he worked had caused him to get lung cancer. My mother continued to work as an editor for a magazine publishing company that was owned by her father. Jiri worked as a mechanical engineer in Branik (just south of Prague) for a company that made medical instruments. Jan and I were still in school, so we weren't able to contribute very much to the household income. The war was beginning to turn our happy lives into a nightmare.

CHAPTER 3

I N 1944, THE Russian offensive intensified, and Jan and I were
drafted into one of the labor camps. I was now sixteen years old.
Due to a shortage of working personnel, most Czech teenagers from the
ages of thirteen to eighteen years were sent to work in forced labor camps
for the Germans. The Nazis used us as free slave labor for their war effort.
We were sent to the eastern front in Poland to dig foxholes and anti-tank
trenches for the German army approximately thirty kilometers from the
Birkenau concentration camp in the town of Oswiecim (Auschwitz).
The winter of 1944 was very cold, and none of us had warm clothing
or good shoes, and yet we had to work very hard or else worry about
getting killed. The labor camp where I was kept had mainly Czech and
Polish teenagers (girls and boys), and we did our best to look out for
each other. Jan was at the same labor camp, but he was assigned to a
different barrack then I was, so I didn't see him that often.

I befriended a Czech boy named Soucek who was the same age as
myself and slept next to me.

"Hi, my name is Julius," I said as I introduced myself to Soucek.

"I'm Soucek. Welcome to the hellhole," he replied.

"How long have you been here?" I asked.

"Four months."

"Where are you from?"

"Prague. How about you?"

"I'm from Prague too. It looks like there are lots of Czech teenagers here."

"There are, and the Nazis keep bringing in more."

"I have a twin brother named Jan, but he was assigned to another barrack. I am going to try and find out which one."

"You might see him during the day at work, but that also depends on what jobs they assign him to."

"Are you able to get any news from your family?"

"No, I haven't received one letter or been allowed to write one myself. They treat us almost as bad as they treat the Jews. The only difference is that they don't kill us."

"How do you know that they are killing Jews?"

"Some of the older boys have been inside the Birkenau concentration camp taking supplies and food from our camp and have seen them getting killed."

"Were they trying to escape?"

"No, I heard that when the Jews arrive at the camp on trains the Nazis force them to undress and go into gas chambers. Then they force the other Jews to burn them in these huge ovens."

"How can that be? Why would they want to kill all these people when they could put them to work?"

"They do keep the strongest men and women alive to work at the camp, but they have no need for the elderly, sick, or the children, so they get rid of them."

"If that is true, how could they possibly keep this a secret from other governments?"

ILONA REINITZER

"Because the Nazis will kill anyone who talks about it. They also threaten to kill your family members just to make sure you don't talk."

"I just can't believe that they are getting away with this."

"Well, they are, and you need to be very careful about what you do and say here because they don't just have Jews in the camp. There are political prisoners and people who spoke against the Nazi party. For that matter, you can be sent there for almost anything."

At first, I didn't quite believe what Soucek had told me. I thought that he was exaggerating or maybe the older boys had lied to him, but I decided I needed to be careful about whom I spoke to and what I said to them.

Soucek showed me around the camp and explained the daily schedule to me. The barracks we stayed in were just large tents and were not heated. We had to get up early in the morning and wash ourselves using buckets of water. We were only allowed to shower once a week. There was only one large shower room for the entire camp, so each barrack would rotate showering on a different day. The shower room was just a tent with large buckets of water and hoses. The air and water temperature was freezing, so we would keep our clothes on and just wash one part of our body at a time.

We ate all of our meals outside where the cooks prepared the food over a large campfire in huge pots. Breakfast consisted of watered down tea, bread, and some kind of hot porridge. We were given soup for lunch and dinner along with bread. The soup never had any meat in it, and the potatoes and vegetables were usually half-rotten. Once in a while, we were given really bad tasting coffee.

After breakfast, each barrack was assigned to different duties. Soucek and I were both assigned to help the mechanics to maintain the German tanks. Jan ended up getting assigned to another section of the camp where he had to dig foxholes all day.

We had to work twelve-hour day with only twenty minutes for lunch. In the evening, we all hung around in our barracks, talking to one another, but usually we were so tired that most of us went to bed almost immediately. We had to sleep on the floor on straw. There were no pillows, and each of us only got one wool blanket. I used the straw to stuff around me to help keep me warm.

After a few weeks, I realized that everything Soucek told me about Auschwitz was all true. I heard the constant sound of the trains going into the Auschwitz camp. There was no way that the camp could hold the thousands of people that arrived each week, so I knew they must be killing the Jews. Also on certain windy days, I could see and smell the black smoke coming from the camp and that was thirty kilometers away.

I only saw Jan about once a week while he was heading toward the area where he had to dig foxholes. There were over five hundred men and women in the camp, so it was hard to locate where he slept at night. I tried to leave my barrack one night to see if I could find him, but one of the soldiers caught me and warned me that I better not leave the barrack again or I might get shot.

Every day Soucek and I would report to the field where all the tanks were kept and had to help the mechanics make repairs and maintain the tanks. One day, some of the older boys refused to work because they said they were not given enough food to sustain themselves in the cold weather. They thought they could go on strike and demand more food, but the soldiers just shot a few warning shots in the air close to them and yelled at them to go to work. The boys scrambled back to work and never complained again.

After about a month of working on the tanks, I learned enough about them to know what would cause them to break down, so I came up with a plan to sabotage them. I hated the fact that the Nazis were keeping me there as a prisoner and wanted to do anything I could to prevent them from winning the war. I decided to ask Soucek to help me since he was the only one I knew well enough to trust.

"I have a plan to try and sabotage the tanks, and I need your help," I told Soucek.

"What kind of plan?" Soucek asked.

"I am going to loosen some of the parts in the engine so that the tank will eventually break down while it is being driven. I need you to keep watch and let me know whenever one of the mechanics comes close," I replied.

"You're crazy. You know, they will eventually figure out that some of us must have sabotaged the tanks, and they will try to investigate who did it," Soucek answered.

"As long as we keep our mouths shut, no one will know we were involved, right?" I asked.

"I don't know. It's risky, and I don't want to end up in Birkenau," he stressed.

"Well, just think of what our lives will be like if the Nazis win the war," I replied.

"All right, I'll help, but don't trust anyone else and don't tell anyone what we are doing," Soucek replied.

"Agreed," I responded.

The next day Soucek stayed on the lookout for any mechanics walking by as I started loosening bolts and engine parts so that the vibration of the engine would eventually cause them to fall off while the tanks were operating. I would only loosen them a little bit so that no one would notice that anything was amiss.

Our plan worked great and soon we started finding ways to sabotage all the machinery a little bit at a time during our normal working hours. We began to notice the mechanics talking about how often the tanks kept getting returned to them for repair. I was thankful that my father had insisted that I take German language lessons since I was a young boy because I was able to listen in on their conversations to get information. I never let on that I knew what they were saying.

Soucek and I continued sabotaging the tanks for a few months until one day one of our workmates overheard one of the soldiers talking about how the tanks were breaking down much more often than they should be and that someone from this camp had to be doing something to them. We all knew they would eventually try to figure out who was responsible.

"Soucek, I just heard from Alexej that the soldiers figured out that someone has been sabotaging the tanks. You know, it is a matter of time before they start interrogating everyone to find out who is involved," I said.

"We better stop messing with the tanks until this blows over," Soucek said.

"I have been thinking, and I think we should try and get the hell out of here," I replied.

"That is very risky. You know, they won't have any problems shooting us if they catch us escaping. They might even put us in the camp with the Jews," Soucek responded.

"I know, but I am sick and tired of being cold, hungry, and overworked. Who knows how long they will make us stay in this camp. The Nazis are insane, and I don't want to wait around to see what they do to us in the future," I pronounced.

"You're right. What's your plan?" Soucek asked.

"I need to try to find Jan and tell him our plan so he can get out of here too," I answered.

"It's going to be hard for you to find him and talk to him without anyone overhearing. You are going to put us at risk of having someone find out that we are planning on escaping," he added.

"I will be careful, but I need to at least try to find him," I responded.

That evening, I snuck out of the barracks and made my way through several of the tents trying to find Jan. I quietly whispered his name and asked the boys if they knew Jan. I was just coming out of the fifth tent when I came out to find a soldier pointing a rifle at my chest.

"What are you doing?" he yelled.

"I am feeling very sick and came out of the barrack because I feel like I need to vomit," I replied.

"Well, get back inside and vomit into a bucket if you have to," he shouted.

I went back inside the tent even though this wasn't my barrack, but luckily, no one said a word. I waited a few minutes and then snuck out the back of the tent and made my way back to my barrack. The next morning I made plans with Soucek on our escape.

"Did you find your brother?" Soucek asked.

"No, I tried but there were just too many barracks, and there were soldiers everywhere. I almost got caught," I replied.

"So what are you going to do?" Soucek asked.

"I guess I will have to leave without him," I replied sadly.

"At least, you can let your mother know where he is and that he is alive," Soucek responded.

"I guess so, but I hate to leave without him. It is getting too risky for us to stay since the soldiers are going to try and figure out who has been sabotaging the tanks," I said.

"When do you think we should try to escape?" Soucek asked.

"We need to leave soon so let's plan on leaving tomorrow evening after it gets dark," I replied.

The next day, the soldiers came into the barracks and told all the workers who had been assigned to tank maintenance that we were now going to be digging foxholes. They must have decided to reassign the workers so they couldn't do anymore damage. Soucek and I decided we better try to escape as soon as possible and not wait until evening.

Soucek and I were out in the field digging holes and came up with a plan to try to go to the barracks to use the bathroom and escape while everyone was still in the fields. Soucek went over and asked the guard first.

"I need to use the latrine. Can I go back to the barracks?" Soucek asked.

"No, you can go over there by that tree," the guard replied.

Soucek looked back at me and then slowly started walking to the edge of the field near the forest. I knew that we wouldn't be allowed to go back to the barracks now but thought that we might be able to make a run for it from the forest.

"I'm feeling really sick. I think I might throw up," I told the guard.

"Well, don't throw up in front of me. Go over there by the trees," he replied.

I started heading over toward Soucek who was now just entering the forest. Soucek was waiting for me, and we quickly discussed what we should do.

"Do you think we can out run them if we go now?" Soucek asked me.

"I don't know. It depends on how long it takes them to notice that we are gone," I answered.

We looked back toward the soldiers and saw that several tanks were pulling out of the maintenance area and heading out toward the field.

"Hey, look, it is going to take some time for the tanks to go by, so this is our chance to make a run for it," I added.

We ran for the first couple of kilometers and then walked through the forests the entire night. We traveled far away from the roads and stayed in the valleys and forests. We heard some tanks and trucks in the distance, but no one came close to us. In the morning, we decided to hide under leaves and twigs in the forest until the sun set so that we wouldn't be seen. It was freezing cold, but the dead leaves helped warm us, and we stayed close together for warmth. The next evening we continued walking and were trying to head west in the direction of Prague, using the stars to navigate by. Just before sunrise, we came to a small farm which was out in the middle of nowhere. We later found out that we were near Rybnicka.

"Look, there is a house up ahead," I whispered.

"What if the soldiers are waiting for us there?" Soucek asked.

"I don't think they are because we haven't heard anything since the first evening. Maybe we should hide out in the woods for a few hours and see if we can figure out who lives there and if there are any German soldiers hanging around," I answered.

We watched the farm from a distance for a few hours and only saw a woman and two small children, so we decided it was safe to approach her.

"Hi, my name is Julius, and this is Soucek," I said, pointing to my friend.

"We were drafted by the German army to help them build a camp, but it is finished now, so they sent us home," Soucek added.

We didn't want to tell her the truth for fear that she wouldn't help us.

"They didn't give us any money or food when we left, so we were wondering if we could trade you some cigars for a meal," I asked.

Soucek had stolen some cigars from one of the soldiers, hoping that we could sell it for some money or trade it for some food.

"My name is Joanka, and these are my two children. I don't have any money to give you, but you can sleep here for the night, and I will give you some food," she replied.

"Thank you so much. We really appreciate it," Soucek said.

We went inside the small farmhouse, and Joanka made us some potatoes with gravy for which we were very grateful for because we were starving.

"I am guessing that you boys are really running away from the Germans because I haven't heard of them letting any of their 'free labor' go home," she said.

Soucek and I looked at each other and didn't know what to say. We needed her help but weren't sure if we could trust her.

"You don't have to worry about me turning you in. I will help out anyone who needs it during this horrible war," she added.

"We did escape from a German work camp approximately thirty kilometers from the Auschwitz concentration camp," Soucek replied.

"We were taken from our families in Prague by the Germans and forced to dig anti-tank trenches and help with tank maintenance," I added.

"My husband was an officer in the Polish army, and he was sent to a German POW camp because of his military resistance against the Germans," Joanka said.

"Have you heard from him at all?" Soucek asked.

"No, it has been months since he has been gone, and I haven't been able to find out anything about how he is doing or if he is still alive," she answered.

"Do you have anyone to help you with your farm?" I asked.

"No, I am alone with just my two children. I had to sell most of the animals and only keep what I could take care of myself," Joanka answered.

"Can we help you do anything before we leave tomorrow?" I replied.

"You better just hide in the basement because there are always German soldiers in the area, and they might see you," she answered.

We hid in the basement of the farmhouse and spent the day sleeping because we knew we would be traveling again that evening once the sun set. We had no idea if the German soldiers were looking for us, but we wanted to get out of Poland as fast as possible.

"Julius, Soucek, it is dark now, so you can come upstairs," Joanka called.

"Can you tell us where the closest train station is?" I asked.

"It is in Rybnik which is approximately forty to fifty kilometers from the Czech border. If you head in a southwest direction, it is about a three days walk from here," she replied.

"We really appreciate you letting us stay here and giving us food," Soucek said.

"I packed you a bag with some potatoes, bread, and water to take with you. I am sorry that I don't have any money to give you for a train ticket," she added.

"You have done enough for us. Here, take these cigars. Maybe you can sell them in town for something you need," I said.

"Keep them. You will need them more than I will. I still have food from my garden," she said.

ILONA REINITZER

"Thank you again for everything you have done for us," Soucek replied.

"Yes, and I hope your husband comes back to you safely," I added.

We said our good-byes and then headed southwest in the direction of Rybnik.

CHAPTER 4

FOR THE NEXT two days, we hid in the forests during the day and walked at night. Occasionally, we ran into a farmer, and they would point us in the right direction to the train station. On the second evening, we found the train station and waited for the next train to come in.

"Julius, look! There's the train station!" Soucek exclaimed.

"We need to find out what the schedule is and which train is heading toward Prague," I replied.

"One of us should go alone and pretend that we are going to visit some relative in Prague," Soucek suggested.

"Good idea, but we need to ask someone at the station which train is going to Prague. If we ask at the ticket counter, they will want to know why we aren't buying a ticket," I replied.

"I'll go because I look younger than you," Soucek said.

"Okay, I will stay here and watch for your signal. Wave to me if it is safe for me to join you," I said.

Soucek left the edge of the forest where I was hiding and made his way to the train station. I watched as he sat down on a bench next to an elderly lady and started to speak with her. After a few minutes, he got up and walked back to where I was hiding.

"What happened?" I asked.

"That lady told me that there is a train heading to the Czech border in two hours from now. I told her I was visiting my grandmother in Przegedza (this was a town we had passed before getting to Rybnik) and was heading back home to Prague, so we needed to know what time the train left," Soucek answered me.

"Did you see any police or soldiers?" I asked.

"I saw two of them inside the building through the window, but they didn't notice me," he replied.

"They are going to inspect the train before it leaves, so we are going to have to hide somewhere other than the passenger compartments," I stated.

Soucek and I hid in the forest and waited until the train arrived. Luckily, it was dark that evening and no one noticed us sneaking along the side of the stopped train. We ran along the train, looking for an empty car that was open but couldn't find any.

"Do you see any cars other than passenger compartments?" Soucek asked.

"Not yet. Maybe we can find a car containing supplies that we can hide in," I answered him.

We made our way down the entire train and realized that this was a passenger train only.

"What are we going to do? The soldiers are going to check all the train compartments. Plus the conductor is going to ask for our tickets," Soucek added.

"I think our only chance not to be seen is to hide on the roof of the train," I stated.

"We are going to fall off," Soucek stressed.

"I don't think we have a choice, so we better take the risk. There are handles on the roof to hold onto," I added.

We went to the back of the train and climbed up the stairs to the top of the roof and lay there quietly for about an hour, listening to the soldiers searching the train. We were hopeful that since the soldiers hadn't found us yet that we were safe. All of a sudden, a bright light was shown on us, and one of the soldiers yelled that he has found two men on the roof of the train. The soldier yelled at us to get off the roof of the train or else he would shoot us.

We were taken by gunpoint to a holding area which was an old damp building that had water running down from the walls. The soldiers tried to interrogate us, but I pretended that I couldn't understand them (they were speaking German). They brought in another worker from the train station to translate, but he realized that we weren't Polish, and that we couldn't understand him either. They finally figured out that we were Czechs, but they didn't know yet that we had escaped from the labor camp outside of Auschwitz.

Once the guards realized that they couldn't interrogate us, they locked us up in a room and left us. We spent the day lying around, locked up in a freezing room with no furniture. No one came to see us for hours, and we did not receive any food, only a little bit of water.

"What do you think they are going to do with us?" Soucek asked me.

"They will probably send us back to the labor camp," I replied.

"What if they kill us for escaping from the camp?" Soucek worried.

"I don't think they will because they could have shot us already. My guess is that they are going to send us back because they need as much free labor as they can get," I added.

"We better get our stories straight in case they interrogate us separately," Soucek stated.

"Let's stick with the story that we are brothers visiting our grandmother in Przegedza, and we were returning home to Prague," I said.

"Good idea, because even if they find the elderly lady I spoke to, our story will be the same as what I told her. Do you think they will believe that since we were hiding on the roof?" Soucek asked.

"We'll tell them that we spent the money our grandmother gave us for the tickets on food, so we thought we would hide on the roof," I answered.

"Let's hope they believe us," Soucek said.

That evening, one of the guards returned with a Polish man who spoke a little Czech. I heard the guard tell him to translate and ask us a few questions. He was told to ask us who we were and what we were doing on the roof of the train. We told him the story that we rehearsed and he translated that to the guard. The guard seemed satisfied with the story, and the two of them left.

We slept on the cold, hard floor that night, but at least, they left us some food to eat and some water. The next morning, the same two guards returned with an SS officer and told us that he knew we had escaped from the labor camp. He knew our names, and even knew that I spoke some German. He also stated that they were now going to send us to the Birkenau camp as punishment for escaping. Then they turned around and left.

Soucek began to panic because he knew what the conditions were like at Birkenau. I was very worried myself, so I started thinking of ways that we could try and get out of this place. A few hours later, the guards returned.

"Let's go you two," one of the guards yelled.

"Where are we going?" Soucek asked.

"Shut up and follow me," the guard replied.

Soucek didn't understand what he said, so I had to translate for him. I told him it would be better if we just stayed quiet, otherwise, we would just make them angry and who knows what they would do to us.

The guards shoved us in a back of a truck where we sat for the next two hours or so. We had no idea where we were going, but we were very scared that we were being taken to Birkenau. When the truck stopped and they opened the doors, we saw that we were back at the labor camp. Soucek and I were instantly relieved. We were taken to the trenches and told to start digging.

That evening, when we were back at our barrack, we found out why we were back at the labor camp and not at Birkenau. One of the other boys told us that the Germans heard that the Russian army was advancing, so they needed as many people as possible to work on fortification of their tank trenches. They were making everyone at the camp dig the trenches. Soucek and I considered ourselves very lucky because if the Germans didn't desperately need these trenches dug, we would have ended up at Birkenau.

We spent the next several days and nights digging trenches. The guards had us work rotating double shifts, so we were all exhausted. We knew that the Russian army was close by when we heard the gun shells in the distance. A few days later, the gun shells began flying over our heads, and at nighttime, the sky was red from the explosions of the guns that they were firing. The camp was now situated right between the German and Russian positions, and for the first time, I could see the frightened faces of the German soldiers. Many of them were only a few years older than me.

A few weeks had passed, and I tried to make friends with the German soldiers, hoping that they would like me, and I would be treated better. It helped that I spoke some German because of the German language lessons I had taken in school as a young boy. During our free time, I offered to play the guitar to entertain the soldiers, so they grew to like me. One night, while I was playing the guitar at the officer's club I was telling the soldiers how exhausted I was and that the next day I was scheduled for a double shift of digging trenches, so they let me go back to my barrack to go to sleep.

The next morning, I awoke to Soucek shaking me.

"What's going on?" I asked.

"We have to help pack up the camp. The Germans are evacuating," Soucek replied.

"Do you know why?" I asked.

"One of the boys told me that he heard some soldiers speaking, and they said the Russians are getting close," he replied.

The guards seemed to be in a panic and were yelling for all of us to hurry up and pack up the tents and equipment. We could hear gun shells all around us, and it seemed to be getting closer. As we were loading up one of the trucks, Soucek and I passed by the tent where the officer's club was. The tent was no longer there, and the entire area was burned.

"I was there last night, playing the guitar. Thank God I asked to leave early!" I exclaimed.

I was very lucky because the next day I was told that the entire club had been destroyed by an underground group about one hour after I had left and everyone inside had been killed.

When the camp was packed up, the soldiers loaded all of us from the labor camp on a train, which was heading west toward Germany. On the train, I found Jan whom I hadn't seen since I returned to the camp.

"Jan, over here!" I yelled. Jan saw me and made his way through the train over to where Soucek and I were standing.

"I haven't seen you in weeks. Where have you been?" Jan asked.

"This is my friend, Soucek. We managed to escape about a month ago but we were captured and brought back here," I replied. Soucek and Jan shook hands.

"Nice to meet you," Soucek said.

"Likewise," Jan replied.

"I heard some soldiers speaking, and they said the Russians are getting close which is why they loaded us on the train. We are heading toward Germany to some concentration or labor camp there," I told Jan.

"We need to get off this train and go back to Prague or who knows where we will end up," Soucek added.

"How can we do that with all the soldiers everywhere and who knows if the train will even stop before we get to Germany?" Jan asked.

Just as the three of us were discussing how we could get off the train, the train was attacked by Russian airplanes (they were called Kotlari). One of the planes hit the engine of the train which caught on fire and exploded.

"Oh my God! The train is on fire!" Soucek exclaimed. There was steam coming out of the engine, and there was fire everywhere.

"We should run to the forest," I replied.

"The soldiers will shoot us!" Jan yelled.

"Look, the German soldiers are running into the forest themselves," Soucek said.

There were about five hundred teenagers like myself on the train, and we had no idea what we should do. We wanted to leave the train, but there were bullets flying all over, and we didn't know if the German soldiers in the forests would shoot at us.

"I think we need to try to make it to the forest too because the entire train is going to be engulfed in flames soon. It could even explode," I added.

We decided to get off the train, and as soon as a few of us started running from the train, all the other teenagers started to follow. I jumped off the train and ran in the opposite direction from where most of the soldiers had gone. I ended up losing Soucek and Jan somewhere back at the train station. There were hundreds of people running everywhere, and the Russians were still firing from the air. It was complete chaos!

Once I was somewhat safe in the forest, I stopped and started to look for Jan and Soucek. There were many teenagers running in different directions, but after about twenty minutes, I found Soucek.

"Have you seen Jan?" I asked Soucek.

"No, I can't believe I was able to find you in all this madness," Soucek replied.

"We need to find him before we can leave here," I declared.

"Well, we can't go back to the train station because we will be killed by either the German soldiers or the Russian Kotlari," Soucek stated.

"Let's head back to the edge of the forest and see if we can find him anywhere," I uttered.

We walked back toward the train station where there will still hundreds of people running past us. Some of them even told us we were crazy to turn back. When we got to the edge of the forest, we could see people lying dead all over the place. The train hadn't exploded, but there was black smoke everywhere which was a good thing because it made it difficult for anyone to see us.

"I don't see Jan anywhere," I said.

"At least, we didn't see him lying dead anywhere," Soucek assured me.

"He probably headed in the opposite direction," I replied.

"Do you hear that?" Soucek asked.

"What?" I responded.

"It's quiet. The Kotlari are gone," Soucek declared.

"We need to get out of here because the soldiers will come back to the train now that the shooting has stopped," I said.

"Don't worry, I'm sure Jan will head back to Prague, and you will find him when you get home," Soucek assured me.

As much as I wanted to find my brother, I knew we had to leave right then, or we would risk getting captured by the German soldiers, so we turned back into the forest and headed toward Prague.

ILONA REINITZER

CHAPTER 5

S OUCEK AND I decided to follow the railroad tracks west toward the Czech border because we knew it would eventually take us into Prague. The train had only travelled about fifty kilometers when it was attacked, but luckily, it was headed in the same direction as Prague, so it brought us a little bit closer to home. Soucek and I walked for two days and had only water to drink from the nearby streams. On the second day, we ran into a troop of Russian soldiers who gave us a little food once they found out that we were Czech teenagers just trying to get home. We continued on toward the Czech border, and the Russian soldiers headed toward Germany. They told us that they were going to Berlin. A few hours later, we finally made it to the Polish-Czech border. We waited until nightfall and then crossed into Czechoslovakia without anyone seeing us.

A few kilometers down the road we came to a train station. We found out that there was a train there that was heading toward Prague!

"Soucek, we need to get on the train," I said.

"Yeah, but we don't have any money, so what do you think we should do?" Soucek asked.

"We are going to have to figure out a way to get onboard or else we are never going to make it home," I replied. I knew that it would take us days to get home on foot, and we didn't have enough food to go that far.

We hung around the back of the train station until we saw that it started to move and then jumped aboard.

"Quick, let's try and find a place to hide," I said.

"The conductor is already coming," Soucek replied.

We tried to duck behind a row of seats, but it was too late, the conductor had already spotted us.

"Hey, what are you boys doing here?" the conductor asked.

"We need to get home to Prague. We were sent to work for the Germans in a Polish labor camp and managed to escape," I replied.

"We don't have any money or food, and we are trying to back home to our families," Soucek added.

"I have a son too that was sent to a German labor camp a few months ago, and I haven't seen him since. You boys can stay on the train, but I have to warn you that German soldiers randomly search the train at different stops before we get to Prague. Do your best to hide and if you are caught, I never saw you," the conductor warned.

"Good luck, and I hope you make it back to your families," he added.

We stayed in the back of the train and pretended to be sleeping so that no one would notice us when they walked by. A few hours later, the train came to a stop in Olomouc, a large city in Moravia, and just as the conductor predicted, the train was searched by German Hitler Youth soldiers. These were soldiers between the ages of fourteen and eighteen. They had all been trained to use their weapons, but they were very inexperienced. The only difference between them and us was that they had guns. One of the soldiers came over to us and asked for our travel documents and passports, but since we didn't have any we were forced to get off the train.

We made up a story about how we were brothers who were trying to get back home from taking care of our sick grandmother in Ostrava (a town close to where we boarded the train). I heard the soldiers discussing what they should do with us. I'm not sure if they believed us or not, but they told us we were going to be put on a train to Poland and taken to a labor camp. The soldier who was interrogating us was only a few years older than me, and he looked tired and scared. I felt bad for him because I knew he really didn't want to be here and was only following orders, so I decided to tell him the truth and try to help him.

"Listen, we just came from a labor camp in Poland, not far from the border and the Russians have already taken over. If you go there, the train will be ambushed, and you could die," I told him. "The best thing you can do is get out of your German uniform, find some civilian clothes, and go back home to Germany," I added.

"How stupid do you think I am? Get the hell on the train now. You're lucky, I don't shoot you right here on the spot," the soldier yelled.

We were put on a train heading back to Poland, which was filled with at least two hundred other Czechs being sent to the labor camps. We were warned that if we disobeyed any of the soldier's order, every second person would be shot.

"Hey, Soucek, look! The train heading toward Prague is starting to leave!" I exclaimed.

"Do you think we can jump on it before getting caught?" Soucek asked.

Our train was right next to the train that was leaving and several of the teenagers were whispering to each other that we could make a run for the train.

"If we all leave, there is no way that the soldiers will be able to stop us all," I replied.

"They did say that they would shoot us if we tried to escape," Soucek stressed.

"How many soldiers do you remember seeing?" I asked.

"Not more than three," Soucek replied.

"I didn't see any more than that either. Plus, they were all around our ages and probably can't even shoot well," I stated.

"That's true. They are very inexperienced, so they aren't going to be able to shoot the majority of us," Soucek assessed.

"Plus, if we make it to the other train, there is no way they can catch up to us," I said.

There were no soldiers in our compartment, so I decided to tell all the other teenagers our plan.

"Listen everyone, the train heading toward Prague is leaving. If we all jump off this train and get on that train, there is no way that the soldiers can shoot all of us," I announced.

"But we have to go right now or the train will start moving too fast for us to get on," Soucek added.

Soucek and I then opened the door and jumped off the train and ran toward the other train. Several of the teenagers in our compartment decided to follow us and as soon as we jumped off, hundreds of other prisoners from other compartments on the train noticed us and joined us. We were right about how few soldiers were guarding the train because as far as we could tell, there were only three German Hitler Youth soldiers guarding the train. They started shooting at us, but most of us were able to get on the train safely. I don't know how many people they killed, but there were over hundred Czechs who made it on the train.

The train conductors and passengers had no idea what was going on and the compartments were chaotic. Several of us were explaining to the train conductors about what had just happened. They could have stopped the train and made us all get off, but since they were all Czech citizens themselves, they told us that we could stay on the train. Since there weren't enough seats for all the extra people onboard, most of us just sat on the floor.

We were very lucky that there were no soldiers on the train, and that it was just a commuter train for passengers. We were told that the train was going directly to Prague without any stops. In a few more hours, I would finally be home.

CHAPTER 6

I T WAS MAY 5, 1945, when we finally arrived in the outskirts of Prague. The train came to a stop before it entered the city, and at first, we were worried that the German soldiers were coming aboard but then found out that the Czech underground was actually stopping the train to look for German soldiers. Members of the underground told us that they needed help overthrowing the German occupation in Prague and were looking for new members.

Soucek and I decided that it would be better to help the Czechs than get recaptured by the Germans, so we decided to join the underground movement. We are assigned to the eastern part of the city and were each given a rifle and a Panzerfaust, which was a German anti-tank weapon. It consisted of a small disposable preloaded launch tube, which could fire a high explosive anti-tank warhead by a single person. I was in charge of a road junction in the Vinohrady section of Prague. Our mission was to stop any German tanks from entering the city.

This was the first day of the Prague uprising by the Czech underground. Czech and British paratroopers had landed at the outskirts of Prague and were working their way toward the inner city. The US Army was about thirty-five kilometers southwest of Prague, but they were not allowed to enter the city due to the Jalta Agreement. We heard that there were German troops assembled at

Václavské náměstí, which was located in the center of the city. They wanted to surrender but only to the regular Czech army and not the underground.

Meanwhile, the Russian Liberation Army (ROA) under General Andrey Vlasov's command was located fifty kilometers northeast from Prague when the Czech underground radioed them for their help. The ROA were predominantly Russian forces who were opposed to the communist regime and allied themselves with Nazi Germany. At first, General Vlasov was reluctant to help but decided to fight against the Germans in order to save his soldier's lives.

General Vlasov's division and Czech insurgents engaged with the Waffen-SS German units that had been sent to level the city. During the final days of World War II, there was a huge battle resulting in the deaths of thousands of people. On the last day of the war, the regular Russian Army arrived; however, the battle was already over. On May 8, 1945, the German Army surrendered to Czech military units.

Due to the predominance of communists in the city, General Vlasov and his army tried to surrender to the US Army, however, they did not want to take in the ROA for fear that such aid would harm their relationship with Russia. Shortly after their failed attempt to surrender to the US Army, most of the ROA was captured by the Russians. Many of the higher-ranking officers were executed for deserting the Russian army, and the lower-ranking soldiers were sent back to Russia for lesser punishments. I felt bad for these soldiers because in my mind they were the true liberators of Prague. Without their heavy weaponry, the underground would never have been able to win the battle with the German army.

The next day, Soucek and I turned in our weapons to the Czech army and planned on finally going home; however, the soldiers were ordering all available boys and men to help bury the thousands of dead people who were lying all over the streets. We were told that we had to bury fifty bodies each before we would be allowed to go home, otherwise, the city could suffer a major epidemic of disease. Trucks were delivering bodies to the Malvazinky cemetery where they were sorted by their nationalities (British, German, Czech, Russian, etc.) Many of the bodies were blown apart, so we had no idea what nationality they were, so they ended up in a separate pile.

Soucek and I dug graves and buried bodies until we reached our quota of fifty people a piece. We were now finally allowed to leave and go back to our families.

"Julius, I can't believe we are actually going home. Half the time I didn't think we were going to make it," Soucek said.

"I'm glad we met, and we need to stay in touch," I replied.

"Let me know when you find out where your brother is," Soucek said.

"I will let you know as soon as I hear. I can't wait to get home and make sure that the rest of my family is safe and to get some real food," I replied.

Soucek and I shook hands, gave each other a hug, and then we each left in the direction of our homes. I walked up another mile until I came to the road I lived on. I ran up the stairs, opened the door and yelled, "Mama, I'm home."

My mother came running and was overjoyed to see me. My older brother, Jiri was also home and told me that he had managed to avoid being sent to any labor camps because he had been sent to work at a factory that manufactured weapons that the Germans needed.

I had been gone for over seven months and was one month shy of my seventeenth birthday. I spent the next few days, telling my family, friends, and neighbors about everything that had happened to me. I also ate just about anything that was in the house. Due to the food shortages in the war, there wasn't that much food available, but it still beat the lack of food I had suffered the last seven months. Jan hadn't returned home yet when I arrived but made it back about two weeks after I did.

Jan told us that after he got off the train and couldn't find me that he ended up going with Russian soldiers toward Dresden, Germany. He didn't want to travel by himself for fear that the German soldiers would spot him and shoot him. He thought it was safer to stay with the Russians. After the war ended, he and several other boys from Prague made their way back home.

CHAPTER 7

IN THE MONTHS after the end of the war, the Russian soldiers were camped out on some of the small islands on the River Vltava. Many of these soldiers were recruited as young men from very isolated villages in Russia. They were uneducated and not used to any modern appliances. Some of them did not even know what a toilet was and used them for washing themselves. They were bored now that the war was over and drank most of the time.

Crime in Prague began to escalate and many of the soldiers were caught raping women, stealing bicycles, motorcycles, watches, and committing other crimes. Soon the soldiers were not allowed to go into the city anymore and had to stay on the islands.

One day when I was returning home from the work, I ran into one of the soldiers. He was obviously breaking the rules by being in the city, so I knew he was up to no good.

"Hey, you, what's your name?" he asked.

"Julius," I answered.

"Well then, Julius, I am a very thirsty man, so I am counting on you to go and get me some vodka," he said.

He had a gun on him, so I decided I better do as he asked. I did not understand his Russian very well and thought that he was asking for voda which means water in the Czech language.

"My house is only a few blocks away, so I can go home and bring you some," I said.

"I will go with you and make sure you don't get lost," he said.

We arrived at my house, and I went to bring him a jug of water while he waited outside.

"Here you go," I said and gave him the jug.

He grinned and took a big sip. After a few seconds, he looked at me fiercely and yelled "What the hell do you think you are doing? I should kill you for insulting me."

"What do you mean? You said you were thirsty and wanted some water, and so I brought you some," I replied dumbfounded.

"You idiot! I don't want water, I want vodka," he yelled as he waved his gun at me.

"Oh, I thought you said voda which means water," I told him.

"Well, now that you know what I mean, go and get me some vodka now," he said.

"I don't have any vodka, and I don't know where to get any either. Since the war ended, it has been as difficult to get alcohol as it was during the war," I replied.

The solder was very upset that I wouldn't be able to get him any alcohol. He seemed almost desperate to have some.

"If you can get me some alcohol, I will give you one of these watches that I stole from the Germans," he said.

He opened up his coat and showed me all the watches he had. He must have had at least hundred different watches in his pockets.

"I can probably find you some red wine but that is the only alcohol I will be able to get you," I told him. I knew that he wasn't going to leave me alone until I found him some alcohol, so I figured I would bring him some wine from my house.

"Yes, that is fine. Go and hurry up," he replied.

I went inside my house and got a bottle of some locally made red wine and brought it back to the soldier. He grabbed the wine and started drinking it.

"Let me pick out one of the watches now," I said.

"You didn't think I was really going to give you one of my watches?" he asked laughing.

"You better give me one," I threatened.

"No, I need to save these watches to sell to some other loser like yourself," he replied.

I was getting really angry and was determined to get a watch from him, so I waited until he took another drink of wine and then grabbed his hand. I managed to get the gun from him which I pointed it at him.

"So who's the loser now?" I asked.

"Give me back the gun," he demanded.

"Open up your pockets so I can pick out which watch I want," I said.

He hesitated for a minute and then decided to do as I asked.

"Here, pick one out but then give me back the gun," he replied.

I picked out the watch that I liked and had him throw it over to me just to make sure he didn't get close to the gun.

"Now get the hell out of here," I told him.

"No, I can't leave without my gun!" he exclaimed.

"Too bad, I'm not giving it back to you so you can turn around and shoot me," I said.

The soldier looked scared and wouldn't leave even with me waving the gun in front of him.

"Please, give me back the gun. If I go back to my unit without my gun, my commander might kill me for losing it," he begged.

I really just wanted him to go away and leave me alone, so I emptied the bullets from the gun and gave it back to him.

"Here, take the gun, but I better not ever see you around here again. I'm sure the police would be happy to tell your commander how you are cheating Czech citizens," I said.

I never did see him again, and by the end of 1945, the Russian army left Czechoslovakia and went back to the Soviet Union.

CHAPTER 8

D URING THE NEXT two and a half years, Prague was prosperous once again. My mother remarried in 1946, and Jiri, Jan, and I all moved into our own apartments. In 1947, I attended the Master Graphical School in Prague, and there I met a girl of my age who was studying photography. Her name was Květa, and she worked at a press office called Melantrich part-time. I also worked at Melantrich as a printer, so we saw a lot of each other at work and at school. Květa had long, blonde hair with big hazel eyes. She was also tall and had long legs. I was instantly attracted to her, so I decided to ask her on a date.

"Květa, are you heading to work after school today?" I asked.

"Yes, how about you?" she replied.

"I am too, so why don't we meet by the front doors and walk there together?"

"Sounds good, see you this afternoon," she said.

I was already waiting for her by the front doors when I saw her come out.

"Hello, here let me carry your books for you," I said.

"Thanks. So how were your classes today?" she asked.

"Good, but I always have so much homework to do and that means another late night after I get home from work," I replied.

"I know what you mean. I never have any spare time. I just go to school, go to work, and then do homework."

"How about the weekends? Do you have time to go and do something fun?"

"I do, but this weekend I need to take some pictures of nature for my photography class."

"I have an idea. Would you like to go on a picnic by the Mouldau River on Saturday? You could take lots of great pictures there."

"That is a great idea. I'm sure the pictures there will be a lot more interesting than taking them in the park which is what I was planning on doing."

"Why don't I pick you up around 10:00 a.m. at your house?"

"That sounds perfect. I will make us some sandwiches."

"Great, I will pick up some pastries for dessert."

We arrived at Melantrich and went to our separate departments.

Květa's parents owned a butcher shop in downtown Prague, and their apartment was located above the shop. I arrived promptly at 10:00 a.m. on Saturday and was greeted by Květa's father, Cestmir.

"Hello, Julius, come on in," Cestmir said as he motioned for me to have a seat in his living room.

"I am pleased to meet you," I replied.

"So I hear you work with Květa at Melantrich," he responded.

"Yes, I am studying master graphics in school, so I am working there as a printer to get experience and to pay the bills, of course," I replied.

"Does that mean you are affiliated with the Czech National Party?" he asked.

I didn't want to answer the question because I had no idea what party Cestmir was affiliated with, and I didn't want him to dislike me, so I tried to be as vague as possible.

After the war, there were four main political parties. There was the National Social Party (supported by the United States), the Communist Party (supported by the Russians), the People's Party (supported by farmers), and the Democratic Party (which was mainly neutral).

During the election in 1946, the Communist Party received 30 percent of the vote, the National Social Party received 27 percent of the vote, the People's Party received 20 percent of the vote, and the Democratic Party received 15 percent of the vote, therefore, there was no majority group in Czechoslovakia.

The United States was pushing Czechoslovakia to accept the Marshall Plan (the European Recovery Program for rebuilding and creating a stronger economic economy for the western European countries) to which Russia opposed. There was no agreement made in parliament to accept the Marshall Plan, causing the National Social Party and the People's Party to leave the Czech National Assembly in the hopes that a new government would be formed. The Communist and Democratic parties took advantage of this situation and overthrew the government thus establishing a communist controlled government.

Melantrich was owned by the Czech National Social Party, so Cestmir assumed that I must be part of the Czech National Social Party since I worked there.

"I try to stay out of politics since the communists took over. I have heard of too many people going to jail just for saying the wrong thing," I replied.

"That is a smart response. You never know who you can trust," Cestmir said.

Just then, Květa came into the room with a picnic basket.

"Oh good, I see you already met my father. Are you ready to go?" she asked.

"Yes, and the weather is perfect for a picnic today," I replied.

I shook Cestmir's hand, Květa gave him a kiss on the cheek, and we left for our picnic. We took the subway to the outskirts of Prague and then hiked a few kilometers to a beautiful spot that my brothers and I had found while camping when we were younger.

"Let's lay our blanket out here under this tree," Květa said.

"I thought you might like this spot because there are so many different flowers in the fields next to the river and the pictures would come out nice," I replied.

"This is an excellent spot. Come on, help me pick out some things to take pictures of, and we can eat later," she said.

We spent a few hours taking pictures and even saw some deer that she was able to photograph. Later, we had our lunch and lay on the blanket, soaking up the warm sun.

"Where was your mother this morning?" I asked.

"Oh, she was at the beauty salon getting her hair done. She usually makes her appointments on Saturday mornings. Sorry, you weren't able to meet her," Květa responded.

"I'm sure I will meet her later when I take you home. By the way, your father asked me what political party I belonged to, and I didn't want to answer because I didn't know what party your family is affiliated with. For all I know he could be a communist," I said.

"I should have warned you the other day. My father hates the communists and works as a recruiter for the Czech National Party. I'm surprised he didn't try to recruit you this morning," she replied.

"Well, that is a relief. I would hate to think that the girl's father that I was dating was in the Communist party," I said.

"Are we dating now?" she asked with a smile.

"Of course, we are. Didn't you think so?" I replied.

She laughed, and from that day forward, we were inseparable. We went to school together, worked together, and spent many hours together on the weekends. I met the rest of her family, and they met mine. We all got along great. Cestmir was always having me bring over my friends so he could try to recruit them into the Czech National Party. Most of the employees at Melantrich were already members, so they got together a lot to discuss politics. One evening, Cestmir brought up ways they could help the Czech National Party.

"I came up with this pamphlet that will inform all the Czech citizens of all the awful things that the communists are up to. It also talks about how to join our party and what they can do to help," Cestmir said.

"You need to get copies made so we can distribute them," a friend named Martin said.

"That is what I wanted to speak to all of you about. Do you think we can get these printed at Melantrich," Cestmir asked.

"I don't think that will be a problem since everyone there hates the communists," Imrich replied.

"We will have to be very careful that only the necessary employees are aware of what we are doing," Cestmir stated.

"If the communists do find out who was behind the pamphlets they would most likely arrest us and send us to one of their 'Kangaroo Courts' for trial," Martin added.

The communist government established Kangaroo Courts where they would deny people their judicial rights in order to expedite their trials. This was just a plot for the communists to execute innocent people that they thought were a threat to the government. Due to these courts, many educated people began to flee the country for fear that they would be prosecuted.

"Especially because the government pays such close attention to what is published at Melantrich since the company is supported by the United States," Imrich said.

"That is precisely why we need to communicate to all the Czech citizens what is actually going on in our country since the communists took over. We need to overthrow the government and to do that we need more members," Cestmir said.

"We no longer have any freedom or rights," Martin added.

Květa and I left while the men were discussing how they were going to go about getting the pamphlet printed and distributed.

"My father worries me with all these things he is doing against the communists," Květa said.

"Don't worry too much. He is very careful about who he speaks to and who he gives any information to," I told her.

The truth was that I completely agreed with Květa. I had heard awful things that happened to anyone who was against the government, but I didn't want her to worry anymore than she already was. I also hated the communist government but did not want to get involved with politics, remembering what it was like at the labor camp. I didn't want to give the government any reason to put me in a prison camp.

"Come on, let's get going or we will be late for the concert," I said, trying to distract Květa from thinking anymore about the meeting her father was having.

During the next two years, Květa and I continued to date and fell in love. We completed our college degrees and went to work full-time at Melantrich. Květa would take pictures for the articles that were printed, and I was promoted to a director and had twenty-two people working for me. My plan was to save up enough money to get a bigger and nicer apartment before I asked her to marry me. Things were actually going very well for me until the summer of 1949 when Jan got into trouble with the communists.

CHAPTER 9

JAN WAS A writer and worked for a magazine publishing company in Teplice (a town north of Prague). He mainly wrote poems and other articles that were artistic in nature. At that time, many writers were contacted by the communists and told what to write, usually involving some type of communist propaganda. Jan was also contacted by the Communist party at his job and told that he could continue writing for the paper as long as he wrote certain favorable articles regarding the Communist party. Jan came to visit me one evening and told me about the pressure he was getting from the communists.

"I hate the Communist party, and I am going to write them a letter, telling them they can go to hell," Jan told me.

"You better not. You know what happens to people who go against the government," I replied. I don't think Jan realized how serious of an issue this was.

"I hate being told what I can write about. Now they want me to write some communist propaganda, and I don't even write articles about politics," Jan said.

"I know. Remember how things used to be when we were kids before the start of the war?" I asked.

"Yeah, like all those times we would go camping or play down by the Moldau. Back then, we didn't have to constantly worry about the government.

"I still remember when Papa would tell us all those scary stories before bedtime and Mama would yell at him because she thought we would have nightmares. Of course, she didn't know that we begged him to tell us the stories. The scarier, the better, I always said."

"Those were the good old days."

"Well, if you want some more good old days, you better keep a low profile and write a couple of articles that the communist want you to or else they will keep harassing you."

Jan didn't like being told what to do, so he wrote a letter, telling the Communist party basically that he would write whatever he wanted to write. They responded by sending Jan another letter warning him that he better write what they wanted him to. Jan responded with another nasty letter telling them no.

A few days later, Jan was in his apartment in Teplice when a friend of his came to see him and warned him that a few men from the communist government were trying to locate him and were planning on arresting him. Jan immediately left and went to a friend's house where he hid for a few days. His friend was getting nervous that Jan was staying there and was afraid that the communists would punish him for helping Jan, so he decided to come back to Prague to stay with me.

I hid him in my apartment for a few weeks until one day as I was returning home from work; the apartment manager told me that a few men came by asking if he knew if there was anyone else staying in my apartment. They also tried to convince him to let them search my apartment. The apartment manager told them that he didn't know and refused to let them in. He said that they should come back later when I would be home. I ran into my apartment to warn Jan.

"Jan, the communists know that you are staying here. You need to leave the country immediately," I warned. I knew the communists would make up some bogus crime and send him to one of those "Kangaroo Courts" where he would most likely be convicted and sent to some prison work camp.

"How do you know?" he asked.

"The apartment manager told me that they were asking if someone else was staying with me in the apartment. They must know you are staying here, and they are planning to come back today. You need to get out of here right away," I replied.

"I will hide out at the train station until nighttime and then go back to Teplice," he said.

"Here, take all the money that I have in the apartment. Put whatever clothes you can fit in this backpack, and I will pack you some food to take with you," I said.

"Tell Mama and Jiri that I will write to them once I make it across the border and let them know where I am," Jan replied. Jan gave me a hug, thanked me for all my help, and ran out the door.

Sure enough, the government officials showed up at my door about an hour later. They asked to search my apartment, so I let them in. They questioned me about Jan, so I told them that I hadn't seen him in weeks. I don't think they believed me, but at least, they left. I did notice some men watching my apartment from the street for a few weeks after that, but eventually, they must have known that Jan was no longer staying with me because they stopped watching me.

Later, I found out that Jan got off the train in Teplice and then walked across the border into Germany without any problems. Teplice was only about ten kilometers from the border, so he didn't have far to go.

A couple of months later, I was at work when some more government officials asked to speak with me. They spent an hour interrogating me with questions about how I helped Jan escape into Germany. I told them that I had no idea where Jan was and that I did not help him. They then showed me a letter that they had intercepted from Jan in which he thanked me for helping him. I made up a story about how I helped him right after the war ended and not for escaping into Germany.

The men told me that they would give this information to their superiors and contact me at a later date. I went home that evening and decided that if they were to question me again, that I would need to leave the country. The communist government was executing thousands of people each year for bogus crimes, and I knew I could be one of them. I went to the bank and took out almost all my money in cash and put it in a backpack along with clothes and some nonperishable food. I hid it in my apartment so it would be ready in case I needed to leave quickly.

I knew that I had to tell Květa, so I asked her to meet me at the park that Saturday for a picnic.

"Julius, you look so serious today. What's wrong?" Květa asked.

"Some government officials came to Melantrich to see me and ask me questions about my brother Jan," I replied.

"What did they ask you?" she inquired.

"They think that I helped Jan escape into Germany because of a letter he wrote me thanking me for helping him. I told them that I didn't know anything about his escape until he wrote me from Germany," I said.

"Did they believe you?" Květa asked.

"I don't think so, which is why I wanted to see you today," I responded.

"You are making me worried now."

"I'm sorry, but I needed to tell you what is going on in case they contact you or in case they put me in prison."

"You can't even think that!"

"You know, that it is possible. If that does happen, I want you to pretend that I am only a coworker of yours and not your boyfriend."

"No, I am not going to do that."

"You have to because if you are also implicated in helping Jan, then they will put you in prison too. Then who will take care of your parents?"

"Maybe my father can use his connections to help you."

"No, don't even tell him because the more people know, the more people the communists will interrogate. If I think that the communists plan on arresting me, then I will try to escape into Germany myself."

"I want to come with you."

"You know, you can't do that. Your parents need you now that they are getting older, and I won't have a job or a place to stay."

"I don't care. I can't even think of losing you."

"It is hard for me too, but maybe it won't even come to that, and if it does, I will write you to let you know where I am. Once I have a job and a place to stay, I will come back for you."

We spent the rest of the afternoon, discussing what we would do if I had to leave. Květa was very sad, and it was depressing having to discuss these plans. In the back of my mind, I knew that the communists would never stop harassing me, and then they would start interrogating my family, friends, and coworkers. If I didn't leave, eventually I would end up in prison.

A few days later, I was working when a friend of mine called me from the front office to tell me that two policemen with guns were waiting to speak with me. I told them that I needed a few minutes to wash off the ink from my hands and then would be right there. Instead, I ran out of the back of the building to my apartment which was only a few blocks away. I grabbed my backpack and went straight to the train station using back roads, so I wouldn't be seen on the main streets.

So without saying good-bye to my family or Květa, I boarded a train, heading to Plzeň, then Klatovy, with a final destination of Nýrsko. Nýrsko is a small town approximately eight kilometers from the German border. This was the closest town to the border and only people with special permits were allowed to head toward the border. I got off the train and walked through the forests, staying out of the way of any cars or houses. I walked most of the night and finally made it to the border where I managed to cross over into Germany without being seen.

CHAPTER 10

I KNEW THAT JAN was in Munich because he had written that in the letter that the government officials showed me when they interrogated me, so I headed in that direction. I stopped at all the refugee camps along the way to see if Jan was there. Finally, at one of the camps near Munich, they told me that Jan had been there but had left the week before for Australia. I was very disappointed and knew it would be impossible to find him now.

I stayed at this camp for a few days, deciding what I would do next when I was lucky enough to meet an old friend of mine, Bohdan, who had worked at the Melantrich press office with me a few years back. He had become a pilot and told me that he had dropped propaganda leaflets from his plane over the city of Prague during the elections for the National Social Party. He was now working for a military intelligence agency for the United States.

He introduced me to a major in the US Army, who was in charge of an intelligence unit in Regensburg, Bavaria. Bohdan put in a good word for me, so the major offered me a job establishing safe houses for US personnel in Czechoslovakia in case there was ever a need to hide in hostile times. After the war, there were many underground groups who were working with the United States, trying to overthrow the communist government. These groups were made up of mainly farmers and small business owners who lost their farms and businesses to the communist government. These people risked their lives when they provided shelter and protection for US personnel, but they thought it was worth it since they had already lost everything they had.

The Americans had treated me very well, and since I didn't have very much money or a job, I figured I might as well take this job. A lot of other people who had escaped into Germany from communist countries were going to the United States. I thought of that since I had always wanted to go there, but I also thought that this job would help me go back to Prague so I could see Květa. I was planning on asking her to marry me and bring her back to Germany with me.

So I accepted the job and went through a security screening process and then endurance training which included communicating through Morse code, survival training, weapons training, demolition training, parachuting, and escape and evacuation training. The training took place in Miesbach, Germany (in the Bavarian Alps).

I noticed that there were several other men from all different countries who had also been recruited and went through the training with me. The training lasted at least three months or longer depending on how urgently the agency needed men to go to a certain country. Czechoslovakia was their number one priority, so I and another Czech, whose name was Radek Tyráček, were given our mission after three months of training.

We were given Czech identification papers, radio equipment, and weapons. We parachuted into Czechoslovakia near the town of Klatovy, which is about twenty-five kilometers from the German border. There we contacted an underground group going by the name of "Survivors." These people were mainly farmers whose farms were confiscated by the communist government. We stayed at this safe house for three months and used our time to train the farmers to fight like soldiers. During this time, we sent and received about twenty-five messages with the major.

During the next year, Radek and I separated to work in different parts of the country with different underground groups. We established safe houses and trained these groups how to fight. We would return to Germany every few months to receive new instructions and report back on what we had accomplished.

CHAPTER 11

THE FIRST OPPORTUNITY I had to go back to Prague was in the summer of 1950. Radek and I were given a mission to go to Prague and train underground groups to sabotage operations in factories that manufactured military equipment and aircraft motors. We rented an apartment in Prague under assumed names and blended in as Czech citizens.

I hadn't seen my family or Květa for almost a year, but I wasn't able to jeopardize our mission and attempt to visit any of them. I was also afraid that their lives would be in danger if someone found out that I had visited them. I hadn't sent Květa any letters either since I had left for the same reason. I realized that as much as I wanted to see her, it was just too dangerous.

A few weeks after Radek and I arrived in Prague, an old friend of mine that I knew from school recognized me while I was walking back to my apartment and ran up to me.

"Julius, it's me, Matus. I haven't seen you in years!" he exclaimed.

"I looked around nervously because I didn't want to answer too many questions. I wasn't quite sure what I should do. Meanwhile, Matus kept right on talking and telling me about all of our old friends and what he had been doing over the last few years.

"So what have you been up to these past few years?" Matus asked.

Matus had known Květa and me when we were all in school together, so I decided to ask him if he knew what she was doing now. I decided to make up a story about where I had been the last few years too.

"I decided to get out of Prague once the communists took over, so I decided to work for an old friend of my brother, Jiri.

"What kind of work are you doing?" Matus asked.

"Believe it or not, but I am helping him run his farm. He owns a farm in Borovany so that is where I am staying now," I replied. Borovany was a small town south of Prague near the Austrian border.

"Somehow, I can't picture you as a farmer seeing as you went to school all those years for graphical arts," he said.

"Well, it seems to be the safest kind of work. There is too much political unrest in the cities plus there is plenty of food to eat," I responded.

"Yeah, as long as you keep it hidden from the communists." He laughed.

"By the way, have you seen Květa?" I asked. "I lost touch with her a few years back. I think she moved," I added. I had no idea where she was or if she had moved but was just making up a story to get any information from Matus.

"The last I heard was that she made it out of the country into England," he replied.

"Why did she go there?" I asked.

"I heard that she needed to get out of the country because of the trouble her father had gotten her family into," he responded.

"What kind of trouble?" I asked. I already knew that he must have gotten in some kind of trouble because of his association with the National Social Party.

"I heard that members of the SNB (Communist National Security Corps) came and interrogated Květa's entire family about her father's involvement with the National Social Party. It turns out that Květa's father was a recruiter for the National Social Party," Matus added.

"How did they find that out?" I asked.

"He was seen handing out pamphlets to people asking them to join the National Social Party," he replied.

"Do you know what happened to her father?" I asked.

"Yes, I ran into her mother last year, and she told me that they gave him a quick trial and sentenced him to two years in prison," he replied.

"That's horrible," I responded. I wondered if he would live long enough to make it out of prison. He was older, and his health wasn't the best. I also knew what kind of conditions that they kept you in while you were in prison.

"Her mother also told me that Květa was afraid that she was going to be arrested because of her association her father, so she contacted members of the resistance to help her get out of the country. That's why she ended up going to England."

"That is awful news," I said. "That's one of the reasons I wanted to get out of the city," I added.

"I know, the government is destroying everyone's life, and if you don't do exactly as they say and agree with their communist ways, then they put you in jail," Matus declared.

Matus and I spent a few more minutes making small talk. I never mentioned my family because he would have been suspicious if I didn't know where they were and what they were doing. I really wanted to ask him several more questions, but it was just too risky, so I said good-bye and made my way back to the apartment that we were staying.

I told Radek what had happened and that made us want to help the resistance even more. The communist government had completely ruined the lives of so many Czech citizens. The next day, Radek and I contacted the underground resistance members, and they set up meetings with workers at the "Walter Factory" in Jinonice, which is a district in Prague. We showed these employees how to destroy tooling and parts without getting caught. A few months later, the government realized that someone was sabotaging the factory and started putting suspected employees in prison. Radek and I knew our situation was getting dangerous, so we had to leave Prague and go back to Germany.

When I got back to Germany, I tried to find out where Květa was. I contacted the International Red Cross, but they did not have any record of her. I also inquired about my brother, Jan, but I couldn't locate him either. I planned on checking back every month or so to see the International Red Cross had found either one of them.

CHAPTER 12

O UR NEXT MISSION was to go to the Slovakian towns of Nitra and Žilina and help two "important" men escape to Germany. This time we decided to cross over the border by foot so we traveled from Regensburg by train to the town of Lam. From there we crossed the border near the town of Nýrsko and picked up our weapons that were stashed in a secret location in an old abandoned building that we had set up during a previous trip. We then continued on to a safe house that was located about sixteen kilometers to the north of us. The safe house was a small farm owned by a man and his wife.

Radek and I decided it would be less conspicuous to travel separately, so we split up at this point. I decided to take the train heading to Bratislava in Slovakia. During the trip, I knew there would be identification security checks, and the first one was right before we reached the city of Brno. I didn't encounter any problems there, and I continued on to Bratislava.

The second security check was near the outskirts of Bratislava. I was in a compartment with five other people, one old man, two children, and two middle-aged women. The police began checking passengers for their identification papers. One policeman came in our compartment to check our papers while another policeman waited in the corridor. He checked all of the other five passengers in the compartment and then asked me for my papers. All of a sudden, the policeman took my ID card and told me that he would be right back. I became really nervous and told one of the women that I was not feeling well and asked to trade seats with her so I could be near the window. The train was already slowing down as we were approaching Bratislava, so I prepared to jump out of the window because I thought the policeman knew my ID card was a fake. I had already started to open the window when he came back in and gave me back my ID card, thanked me for waiting so long and left the compartment.

I got my confidence back again and boarded the next train heading toward the town of Nitra. Once I arrived there, I went to the assigned safe house and contacted the men that I was helping to escape into Germany. Radek arrived at the safe house a few hours after I did.

"How was your trip? Did you have any problems getting here?" I asked Radek.

"I didn't encounter any problems, but I was nervous a few times when the security guards checked my fake ID," he replied.

"How about you?" he added.

"I had the same experience. I almost jumped out one of the train windows when I thought the security guard recognized that my ID was a fake." I laughed.

"Are the men here yet?"

"Yes, I already checked in with them and told them that we were leaving first thing in the morning," I answered.

"Great, let's hope our trip back is as easy as getting here was," Radek responded.

We were preparing to leave as soon as the sun had come up the next morning when the two "important men" came and told us that they weren't going to go with us to Germany. They were scared and decided not to take the risk of getting caught. Radek and I had no idea who these men were and why the Americans wanted to help them escape into Germany (we were only given as much information as we needed to complete the mission). I tried convincing them that we had crossed the border several times already and had never been caught, but they refused to go. The men left the safe house, so Radek and I decided to split up again and travelled back to Germany separately. I headed back to Nýrsko, switching trains approximately every one hundred kilometers until I arrived back to the small (safe house) farm I had first stayed at. The next morning, I left on foot and crossed the border into Germany without incident.

CHAPTER 13

O UR NEXT MISSION was in December 1950, and we were given the task of obtaining plans of prison camps and other secret industrial materials, which were needed to help prisoners escape from these camps. Radek and I decided to cross of the border at a different location so that we would not be recognized riding on the same trains all the time. We crossed the border south of the town, Furth im Wald, on the German side, heading into Všeruby on the Czech side.

The first thing we did was stop at a safe house to pick up our guns (we each got a pistol and a submachine gun). We thought it would be better to travel at night, so we left as soon as we had our guns. We reached the outskirts of Všeruby when we decided to hide out overnight in a cemetery. The problem was that it was a very clear night, and there was a full moon, so we thought we would be too visible to continue on.

The cemetery wasn't our favorite place to camp out, but we knew that no one would be visiting there at nighttime, so it was a secure place to hide. We were hoping that by the next evening it would be cloudy so it would be easier to travel without being seen. We hid in the forest surrounding the cemetery the entire day and waited for the sun to go down. It was just as clear this evening as it had been the night before, so we decided to take our chances and leave our hiding spot in the cemetery rather than waste any more time waiting for better conditions to travel in.

We left the forest and had to cross a clearing in the middle of the cemetery when all of a sudden we heard dogs barking and saw lights. We started running and just about halfway through the clearing, flares were fired into the sky by the Czech border police. The entire sky lit up and the cemetery was as bright as daytime. We could see the border police coming toward us, and they began shooting their machine guns and rifles at us. There were bullets flying everywhere. Radek and I found a small depression in the clearing that we hid in to avoid being hit by the gunfire. We fired back at the border police as long as we could but soon realized that we were severely outnumbered. I felt a stabbing pain in my right leg and when I looked down, I saw that my pant leg was completely soaked with blood. I looked over at Radek and noticed that he had blood pouring from his face.

"Radek, you've been hit. How bad are you hurt?" I asked.

"I don't know, I can't feel my face," he replied.

"My leg was hit," I responded. "I think I can still try to make a run for it though, if you can get up," I added. Radek didn't respond and then I saw that his eyes were rolling upward.

"Radek, wake up, we need to get out of here," I whispered. He mumbled something back, but I couldn't understand him.

I heard more voices and dogs barking. I also heard motorcycles and people everywhere. Then I heard the border police calling for more back up. One of them yelled out to the police who were just arriving, "They are armed, so don't go any closer to them, or they will kill you."

I looked over at Radek and saw that his entire chin was blown off, and that he was drifting in and out of consciousness. We had run out of ammunition, and I wasn't able to carry Radek since I was injured myself, so we stayed in that small depression until the sun came up.

By then Radek wasn't responding to me at all and was lying next to me half-dead. I decided we needed to surrender or else Radek would die from blood loss. We didn't really have a choice since we were outnumbered, completely surrounded by the police, and didn't have any ammunition left. I yelled over to the soldiers (in Czechoslovakian) that I was surrendering.

"Put down your guns and get your hands up over your heads," one of the soldiers yelled.

"My friend is unconscious," I yelled back as I put down my gun and put my hands over my head.

"Walk over here very slowly," he demanded.

I did as he instructed, and when I was out in the open, two of the police grabbed me and took me to their guardhouse to interrogate me. They carried Radek and took him somewhere else since he was unconscious. When we got to the guardhouse, the border police turned me over to several soldiers from the Czech Communist Army. The soldiers threw me down on the floor and at least ten of them started kicking me. They kept asking me what I was doing in the cemetery and who we were working for. I wouldn't answer, so they kept beating me up.

Suddenly, the door opened and an older man came in. He was a major in the Czech Communist Army. He told the soldiers that they were animals and that this was no way to treat a prisoner. My leg was bleeding heavily by now, so I took off my underwear and used it to wrap it around the wound to stop the bleeding. The major told the guards to leave and bring back food and cigarettes for me. I didn't smoke but saved the cigarettes in case I needed them to bribe someone later on.

The major was very nice to me and acted as if he was my friend. I knew enough about interrogation techniques to know that he was just doing this to get information from me. He began to ask me several questions, so I decided to make up a cover story so that they would stop beating me. I knew that I would be punished for this crime but also knew that it would carry a much lighter sentence than the real mission that we were attempting.

"So what is your real name?" the major asked. We had our real ID's with us but also our fake ID's that had a different name.

"My name is Julius Reinitzer," I replied. I decided to tell them my real name because I knew they would find out once they checked the IDs anyway. This way they might believe the story I was telling them.

What is your friend's name?" the major asked.

"His name is Radek Tyráček," I said.

"What were you doing in the cemetery with your weapons?" he asked.

"We were crossing into Czechoslovakia and were paid to help some important men escape into Germany," I replied.

"Who were these men?" he inquired.

"I don't know. We were going to be given this information once we arrived at the train station in Všeruby," I answered.

"Who was going to give you this information?" he asked.

"I don't know who the contact person is. All I know is that we were supposed to go to the train station in Všeruby and wait for someone to approach us," I replied.

"Who are you working for?" the Major inquired.

"I don't know that either. I was living in Ingolstadt (Germany), working as a janitor when I was approached by some German men who wanted to know if I wanted to make a lot of money in a short amount of time," I said.

"I agreed because I was barely making enough money to pay the rent, so I decided to take the job," I added.

"What is a nice Czech citizen, like you, doing living in Germany in the first place?" he asked sarcastically.

"I got in some trouble with the communists last year, so I escaped into Germany so I wouldn't go to prison," I responded.

"What kind of trouble?" he asked.

"I was hiding pigs on a farm where I worked, and I didn't give them to a government official who wanted some pigs for a party he was having," I lied. I was just making up anything that came to my mind.

"How long have you been living in Germany?" he continued asking.

"I escaped in 1949, and this is the first time that I have been back to Czechoslovakia," I replied.

"So you don't know who you are working for and you don't know who you are supposed to be helping. You are just a farmer and a janitor, but yet you were caught with an American weapon which you know how to use," the major stated. The submachine guns we had on us were made in Czechoslovakia, but the pistols were American made.

"Well, the Germans who paid me to take the job did train me on how to use the guns before sending me on this mission," I replied, trying to sound believable.

"And what do you think the Germans were doing with American weapons?" he asked.

"I have no idea. Maybe they were working for the Americans. I didn't ask any questions. All I wanted to do is make some money," I added.

The major stopped being "nice" and was starting to get angry because he couldn't get any more information out of me and knew that I had to be lying. He left the room and spoke to the other soldiers who were waiting outside. I listened at the door and overheard one of the soldiers telling the major that Radek had died. I felt very bad for him but knew that his death probably saved my life. Now that I was the only one alive, they couldn't verify if my cover story was true or not. I heard the door lock, and they left me alone in the interrogation room. I was hungry, thirsty, and in a lot of pain.

The next day, the major and a few other soldiers came back in to see me. This time they brought me some water, food, bandages, and some new clothes. I had no idea why they were being so nice all of a sudden.

"Good morning, Julius," the major said. "I hope you had a nice evening," he added while the other soldiers laughed.

I didn't say a word but began to drink and eat as fast as I could before they decided to take away my food.

"We are going to take you to the train station in Všeruby and see if you are contacted by the people that you say are supposed to give you the instructions as to who you are helping escape into Germany," he announced.

I tried not to show any emotion while I ate my food so that I wouldn't reveal the fact that I knew no one was going to show up at the train station. After I ate, one of the soldiers cleaned my wound and bandaged my leg so that the blood wouldn't seep through onto my new pants. I guess they figured that if I looked injured, the contact person wouldn't approach me. Once I was cleaned up, they drove me to the train station in Všeruby. They dropped me off about one kilometer away from the station.

"You are going to go to the train station and follow the instructions exactly as you were told to do. We will be watching you, so don't think you can try and escape," the major told me. "If you do, we will shoot you, and this time it won't be in the leg," he added.

I walked the one kilometer to the train station and sat down on one of the benches. Since I knew no one was coming to contact me, I sat there and tried to figure out what I should do next. Of course, even if I had a contact person meeting me, they would have figured out that something was wrong because my eyes were swollen and I was bruised all over.

I knew that I couldn't run away, so I just sat there on the bench. After about three hours, the soldiers came back, dragged me into their truck, and took me back to the guardhouse.

"You are a liar!" the major exclaimed.

"No, the contact person didn't show up because I was there a day late," I declared.

"I'm not stupid. I know that they will wait for you every day even if it takes a few weeks," he stated.

"Well, even if they were there, my face was swollen, and I have bruises all over. They would have known that something was wrong," I expressed.

"That is nothing compared with what you are going to look like by tomorrow," he yelled. "Get him out of here and take him to Plzeň," he added, speaking to the soldiers standing next to me.

The next day they transferred me to a jail in Plzeň for further interrogation. Over the next several days, they performed all kinds of different interrogation techniques on me. First, they locked me in a footlocker and left me there for about twenty minutes. I didn't feel any pain at first. It was mainly just uncomfortable until my legs and arms fell asleep. When they opened the footlocker, I couldn't move to get out. When I was finally able to move my arms and legs, the guards told me that since I hadn't left yet that I must want to have another type of torture performed on me. Then they poured ice-cold water on me and then boiling hot water. They gave me electrical shocks and made me climb stairs, causing me severe pain from my injured leg.

When torturing me didn't work, they decided to plant decoy prisoners in my cell to see if I would talk to them and give them any information. I later found out that there were hidden microphones in the electrical outlets outside of the cell. They put a very friendly prisoner on my cell who told me all kinds of stories about everything he had done to sabotage the communist government. I knew he was just a decoy and was trying to get me to trust him, so I would tell him everything that I knew. I knew I couldn't trust anyone and just kept sticking to the same story that I told over and over again.

I also found out that they thought I was part of an underground group called "The Revengers," who were working outside of Plzeň. Most of the members of this group had relatives who were executed or imprisoned by the communist government. Radek and I had heard of this group and knew that they also worked with the espionage agency in Regensburg. They had different safe houses than our group, and one of them was located a short distance from where the border police had captured us. This made them think that we were part of "The Revengers." If the police could connect me with this group, it would have been an automatic death sentence for me since some of their members had been captured and had been sentenced to death by hanging.

Meanwhile, my leg began to heal by itself. I never did get medical treatment or stitches for the wound, but I kept it as clean as possible and used some of my drinking water to clean the wound and the bandage everyday so that my leg would not get infected. I knew that I was very lucky and that I could have died if my leg became gangrene.

Eventually, they took me out of solitary confinement and put me in with the rest of the prison population. I was kept in a cell by myself, but once a day at lunch time, I was able to speak with other prisoners and learn what they had done to be in prison.

"So you are the newest victim of our lovely government," a man named Venceslav said.

"What did you do?" another man by the name of Nikola said.

"Nothing, the communists mixed me up with someone else," I answered.

"Oh sure, just like the rest of us," a Czech military colonel by the name of Patrik responded.

I wasn't sure who I could trust yet so I wasn't about to admit what I was in prison for.

"Let me tell you what 'nothing' that I did to get a two-year sentence. I had a hobby keeping bees and would make some extra money, selling the honey," Venceslav said.

"How did they get you in trouble?" I asked.

"The communists wanted me to give them all the honey and when they found out I kept some of it, they arrested me," he answered.

"That's ridiculous," I responded.

"Just about as ridiculous as my arrest," Nikola said.

"What did you get arrested for?" I asked.

"I am a veterinarian and accepted a pig from a farmer as payment for my service, and now I am stuck in here for two years just like Venceslav," Nikola said.

At that time, all pigs had to be turned over to the government due to meat shortages. Of course, the government officials didn't give the meat back to the Czech citizens but kept it for themselves.

"At least you are young enough to make it out of here," Venceslav responded.

"Don't be silly, you are going to get out of here," Nikola replied.

"I am a sick seventy-six-year-old man. Every day I feel death getting closer and closer, but at least, I will be going to a better place than this," Venceslav said.

"I am with you, my friend. My sentence is ten years, and I will never make it out of here alive," Patrik stated.

"You all have to think positive or else you will die for sure," I replied.

"Yes, you are young and strong and might make it out of here but most of us won't. Look at my incision on my stomach. It is infected and soon I will die. Either that or my stomach cancer will kill me," Patrik said.

"How did you get that incision? Did the guards cut you?" I asked.

"No, I was arrested while I was in the hospital undergoing surgery for my stomach cancer. They took me right off the operating table, and I haven't been able to get any clean bandages or see a doctor who could give me some medication," Patrik answered.

Now I felt really lucky that my wound had healed on its own.

"Why did you get such a long sentence?" I asked.

"A friend of mine immigrated to the United States, and we exchanged letters that the communists intercepted," Patrik replied.

"That is ridiculous. Why would you be arrested for that?" I asked. I, of course, knew the answer to my question but was just playing along in case anyone listening decided to give this information to the guards. I always made sure that I stuck to my cover story no matter who I spoke with.

"Who knows? They either assumed that I had helped him escape or they decided that I was planning on escaping," he replied.

I realized now that it was a good thing that I left for Germany the day the communists showed up at Melantrich. I would have been arrested for sure now that I heard all the stories from these men. The government was arresting citizens for absolutely nothing. I didn't tell these men the real story why I was in prison for fear that they would tell the guards if they were interrogated and tortured. The less anyone knew about me, the better.

The guards continued interrogating me several times per week, and they continuously tried to get me to confess that I was working for the United States and had crossed the border several times but I just kept sticking to my original story. There was no way I was going to give them any information that would hurt the Americans. From what I had seen in the past several years, the United States was the only country that was going to help return things to normal for all the Czech citizens.

Everything that I said was typed and recorded so they could keep track of the details I gave. One guard kept insisting that I had crossed the border and that I needed to tell him what towns I stayed in and where the safe houses were. Finally, after I was severely beaten, I named several towns, none of which were true. He kept asking me to name more towns, but I ran out of town names so I told him to just write down whatever towns he liked best. He was furious and realized that I was just making up names. They finally brought me back to my cell, bleeding and half-unconscious.

CHAPTER 14

AFTER FOUR MONTHS of interrogation, the police gave up torturing me since none of their techniques worked, and I kept sticking to my cover story. I was transferred to the Pankratz prison in Prague to await trial.

There were three types of prisoners at Pankratz. The first types of prisoners were considered political prisoners who disagreed with the communist government. These prisoners wore uniforms with white sleeves. The second types of prisoners were political prisoners who collaborated with the Hitler regime during World War II, and they wore uniforms with green sleeves. The third type of prisoners were anyone who committed a serious crime such as murder, rape, theft, etc., and they wore uniforms with red sleeves. Many of the "red sleeve" prisoners were communists and were put in cells with the political prisoners in order for them to try to obtain information that they could pass along to the prison guards. If they gave any important information to the communists, their sentence would be reduced.

Life was just as bad at Pankratz as they had been at the first guardhouse that I had been kept. Most of the guards were cruel and treated the prisoners horribly. You could constantly hear screaming and crying coming from the tortured prisoners. Several times a week, prisoners were dragged from their cells and executed.

I was considered a political prisoner and was actually treated a lot better than any of the German "green sleeve" prisoners. Many of these prisoners were tortured daily. Some were tied up and doused with boiling water. Some were beaten until their bones broke. These prisoners were given less food than the political prisoners and some died from starvation. None of them received any medical treatment and many died from their wounds.

I shared a cell with a man who had been a fire chief in Prague during World War II. He had recommended that the Gestapo pump water into a Protestant Church in Prague (called the Church of St. Cyril and St. Methodius) in order to drown the Czechoslovakian resistance fighters hiding in the crypt. It was a coincidence that he was my cell mate because I actually witnessed this tragedy myself.

It was June 18, 1942, and I was walking by Resslova Street when I noticed hundreds of SS and Gestapo units surrounding the church. I later learned that Sergeant Jan Kubiš and Sergeant Josef Gabčík were among the seven men in the church crypt. These were the men who three weeks earlier had assassinated Reinhardt Heydrich. Three of the men died as SS soldiers stormed the church, but four of the men continued to fight from the crypt. The Nazi troops spent hours, trying to force their way into the crypt of the church, using tear gas and grenades, but they were unable to penetrate the thick walls.

After hours of shooting and a long stand-off, my cell mate gave the Gestapo the idea to flood the crypt with water, hoping to drown the men. In the end, all the attempts to get the resistance fighters to surrender failed, and the men finally decided to take their own lives.

I let my cell mate know that I wanted nothing to do with him, so he stayed out of my way. Most of the other prisoners wouldn't speak with him either. He ended up being sentenced to prison for twenty-five years.

One of the prisoners that I befriended, named Roman, warned me about one of the guards who watched over my cell block. Roman told me that this man was not only violent but also crazy. His name was Gustaw Boros, and he wanted us to address him as Colonel Boros even though we knew he wasn't a colonel. We nicknamed him Colonel Crazy. He would insist that prisoners jump up when he walked by and shout our names and prisoner number. Each weekend we had to stand at attention and wish him a good weekend. If he didn't think we were sincere enough, he would beat us until we bleed.

"Watch out, Julius! Here comes Colonel Crazy," Roman warned.

I jumped up and saluted Boros as he walked by. I shouted out my name, prisoner number, and wished him a good weekend. Boros didn't like me from the start. He could probably tell that I hated him. He would always stop by my cell and look me over trying to find fault with something that I did so he could punish me. This day wasn't any different.

"Prisoner Reinitzer, why are your clothes dirty?" Boros asked.

"I am very sorry, Colonel Boros, sir, but I have not been allowed to visit the laundry for a change of uniform since I arrived here," I answered.

"That is a lie! We take good care of our prisoners here at Pankratz," Boros yelled.

He then opened my cell, grabbed me, and started to beat me. I ended up with a black eye and bruises all over my body. I was sore for over a week.

"Let that be a lesson to all of you. I expect everyone to have clean uniforms in the future," Boros ordered.

Of course, I still wasn't given a clean uniform after his attack, but he forgot all about that issue the next day and would rant about something else. A few days later, we were eating lunch in the prison cafeteria when Boros walked in.

"Uh oh, Boros looks especially crazy today," I said.

"Just keep your head down and don't look at him," Roman replied.

Luckily, Boros walked past our table and stopped at a table with new prisoners. He would always like to make sure that any of the new prisoners knew who was in charge at Pankratz and make sure that they were afraid of him.

"You there, what is your name?" he asked.

"Prisoner Lubas, sir," he replied.

"What crime did you commit?" he asked.

"One of my dogs bit an important member of the communist party, so they told me to kill the dog, but I couldn't do it. They told me that if I didn't kill the dog that they would put me in prison," Lubas replied.

"So your dog is more important to you than an upstanding citizen of the Communist party?" Boros asked.

"No, Colonel Boros, sir," he replied.

"Just think, your dog is now living a better life than you are because of your stupidity," Boros commented.

"No sir, because they killed my dog anyway," Lubas replied.

"Well, since you seem to like dogs so much, I think I will make you my new dog," Boros said.

Boros grabbed his dinner tray and threw it on the floor.

"From now on, you will eat like a dog using only your mouth," Boros told him.

Lubas looked at him in shock and didn't move.

"Didn't you hear me? Get down on your knees and eat up!" Boros yelled.

Boros then grabbed his stick and began to beat Lubas until he did as he was told. Each day, Lubas had to eat like a dog on the floor and bark at Boros when he walked by. Boros even pet his head and spoke to him as if he really was his pet dog. He was insane!

One morning, I awoke to screams coming from someone a few cells away. Boras and a few other guards dragged one of the prisoners out into the corridor for everyone to see and then started to beat him. The beating took place right in front of my cell. I didn't know the prisoner or what he had done, but they were really angry with him. The man seemed frail and had a small frame. Boros grabbed his guard stick and beat him so severely that he broke his leg in half. I heard the snap and saw his leg hanging on by just the skin. The man kept screaming for him to stop over and over again, but Boros kept on hitting him like some mad man. Finally, Boros gave him a blow to his head so severe that it killed him.

Later, I found out that the prisoner had been sick and didn't get up to stand at attention when Boros walked by which caused him to become enraged. You never knew what would make Boros snap. One Friday, Boros walked by and after I had wished him a good weekend, he hit me over the head.

"What about my wife and children?" he asked.

"Screw them!" I replied.

I knew I was getting a beating anyway, so I just snapped. It was a dumb thing to do but I just lost control of my temper.

"What the hell did you just say?" Boros asked.

He didn't bother to wait for a reply and started to beat me. At some point when I couldn't move anymore, he stopped and motioned for a few other guards to drag me to a dark isolation cell. He probably would have killed me, but I hadn't had my trial yet, so he had to be careful until I was actually convicted and sentenced.

I had no idea how long he was going to leave me here. The cell was completely dark, and I found out that there was nothing in the room by crawling around and feeling with my hands. I was bleeding and in such pain that I couldn't stand up, so I just lay there on the cold concrete floor. I finally passed out and when I awoke, I had no idea how long I had been asleep or if it was even the same day. I was still in a lot of pain, so I just sat there on the floor and tried to think of pleasant thoughts to keep my mind occupied. I dozed off when I heard the door open and a light shine through. I was excited because I thought I could go back to my normal cell, but the guard just put down a glass of water and some stale bread and shut the door again.

"Hey, wait!" I shouted, but no one answered me.

I was starving and very thirsty, so I ate the bread and drank most of the water. I saved a little bit even though I was dying of thirst. Days went by, and I lost track of how long I had been in the cell. The problem was that I couldn't tell if it was night or day or how long I had been asleep. I guess the only good thing about being beaten was that it made me sleep a lot, so it helped pass the time away. Once a day, the guard would bring me the stale bread and only one glass of water. The bread had mold on it, and the water smelled bad. I was completely dehydrated and lost several pounds. I could tell because my pants were falling off me. When I was awake, all I could think about now was how thirsty I was. I didn't even care how bad the water was. I just wanted to stop feeling so thirsty.

Every time I awoke, I made myself get off the floor and walk around the cell so that my muscles wouldn't stiffen up. My body was still swollen from the beating I received, but each day, it would get a little better. I tried to think of positive things to keep my mind occupied so I wouldn't go insane. One day, I started to sing every song that I knew just to keep my mind working. Another day I would think of playing chess with my father and come up with the moves in my head.

I thought of Květa and wondered where she was and what she was doing. I remembered all the great times we had during the years after the war and before the communists took over. I thought of my mother and older brother and hoped that they weren't being punished by the communists because of my brother and me. I thought of my father who died of cancer and remembered how artistic he was. He painted pictures as a hobby, and he was very talented. It made me sad to think of how he died on Christmas day at such a young age.

The one thought that I had every single day since I had been imprisoned was thinking about how I was going to escape. I knew I couldn't live the rest of my life in prison, so I was determined to escape, even if that meant I would be killed trying.

Finally, one day Boras opened the cell door.

"Well, well, Prisoner Reinitzer. Have you learned your lesson yet?" Boras asked.

I couldn't see a thing because the light was too bright, but I knew it was Boras from his voice.

"Yes sir, Colonel Boras," I replied.

I was so thirsty and hungry, and I would have told him anything he wanted to hear. I also knew that if I wanted to make it out of prison alive, I would need to stop getting in trouble.

"Very well then, you can go back to your cell," he said.

"Just remember that if you disrespect me again, I will kill you," he added.

One of the guards escorted me back to my cell. I was still limping and had to keep my eyes shut. Luckily, Roman was in the adjacent cell from mine and saved me some food and water from the cafeteria.

"Julius, put your hand out of the bars, and I will pass you over some food and water," Roman said.

"Thanks!" I exclaimed as I drank every last drop of water and inhaled all the food.

"We were worried that Colonel Crazy killed you when you didn't return for so long," Roman said.

"How long was I gone for?" I asked.

"Fourteen days," he replied.

"You really pissed him off. Usually, he only puts prisoners in the isolation cell for seven days," my cell mate (the ex-fire chief) added.

"Yeah, well, I need to get out of this place soon or Boras is going to kill me one of these days, just like he did to Lubas," I replied.

CHAPTER 15

I MANAGED TO KEEP out of trouble for the next month until I finally went to trial. I arrived at the courthouse and was handcuffed to one of the benches. I noticed that there were several men ahead of me who were also having their trial. I also noticed that each man spoke to their attorney for only about five minutes before their trial began. There was no jury and only one judge who made all the decisions.

Every single person before me ended up getting a guilty verdict. The only difference was the length of the sentence and where the person would serve out their sentence. I knew I was doomed. When it was my time to speak with the attorney, I tried to give him the facts of my case, but he was barely listening.

"How can a judge decide on my case if I can't give you the details?" I asked the attorney.

"Look, no one in this court room is going to be set free. This court hearing is just a formality," he replied.

"How can you live with yourself knowing that you could be helping send innocent men to prison?" I asked.

"I have no choice. If I don't cooperate with the judge, then I will go to prison myself," he replied.

"What is taking so long?" the judge asked my attorney.

"Sorry, Your Honor. We are ready to begin," he replied.

"The report shows that the prisoner was working with the American government to provide them with information to help overthrow the communist government. How does the prisoner plead?" the judge asked.

"Guilty, Your Honor," the attorney responded.

"What? I don't want to plead guilty!" I yelled.

"Keep quiet or else I will sentence you immediately," the judge replied.

"I wasn't working for the Americans," I lied.

"The evidence in this report states otherwise, therefore, I am sentencing you to fourteen years of hard labor in one of the uranium mines," the judge declared. "That should give you plenty of time to think about how you betrayed your government and your people," he added.

I didn't think that very many people (especially those not employed by the government) would have felt betrayed by my "crime."

The entire trial was a joke! My trial lasted less than ten minutes and when it was over, I was put on a bus with several other prisoners. The bus would wait outside the courthouse until it was full and then it would transport the prisoners to the work camps. The government needed workers for all their work camps, so they had already decided what our fates were before we even entered the court room.

The bus headed to a uranium mine in Jáchymov, which is located in western Bohemia (now part of the Czech Republic). There were at least thirty concentration camps in Jáchymov with approximately one thousand prisoners in each of them. I was assigned to a new concentration camp called "Camp Eduard." I found out that criminal prisoners were actually managing the camp under the supervision of guards. The manager of our camp was a criminal by the name of Jenicek. During World War II, he was a police chief in Prague and was responsible for sending many Czech citizens to German concentration camps. Now he was treating the prisoners at Camp Eduard the same way he had when he was police chief. He had the same power and could decide who would be punished and how. Prisoners were scared to talk to each other for fear that whatever they said would get back to Jenicek.

It was difficult figuring out who I could trust and who I couldn't. The worst prisoners to trust were the smokers. They would give up any information for the promise of a cigarette. I was glad I had never picked up the habit of smoking, so I didn't have to deal with any nicotine withdrawal symptoms.

Prisoners who had family nearby were also untrustworthy. They would inform the guards of any information they knew of so that they would be allowed to visit their wife and children. There were even political prisoners who would give guards information for the promise of an early release from prison, however, as long as I was at the camp I never knew of anyone getting discharged earlier than expected.

After a few weeks, I figured out which men could be trusted, and I made a few friends with those prisoners. I met a man named Josef who became my best friend in the camp.

He was twenty-five years old, and I was now twenty-three. In 1948, when the communists took over Czechoslovakia, he had openly spoken against the government and, therefore, was arrested and interrogated. He was convicted of persuading other citizens to resist the communist regime and sentenced to twenty-five years in prison.

When I first met Josef, he was very depressed and spoke of dying a lot. He seemed to have given up on life because he thought he would never get out of this horrible place. The first thing that I did was to convince him that we were going to find a way out of this hellhole. I knew that the minute you gave up on trying to escape that you would never make it out of here alive. I had seen other men give up on their will to live and many of them did die. Some from sicknesses and most of them were killed by the guards because they wouldn't work hard enough anymore.

Within a few weeks, I had him completely convinced that we were going to escape and he snapped out of his depression. It was a good thing too because the only way to survive was to be optimistic.

ILONA REINITZER

The town of Jachymov where the uranium mine
Camp Eduard was located

MINE EDUARD

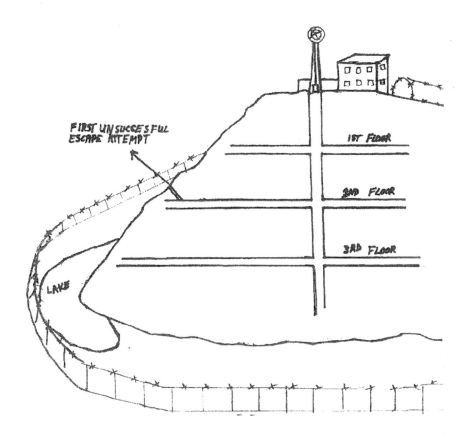

Sketch of Camp Eduard (the uranium mine)

CHAPTER 16

I T WAS NOW July 1951. Josef and I had become familiar with the layout of the camp and were continuously looking for ways to escape. It was hard working in the uranium mines, and the worst part was that we were exposed to the radioactive material without any protective gear. One day, after a few months of working in the mine, we discovered some old mine shafts that were not used. When we worked, we had to lie in a prone position, and from this angle, we noticed small rays of light coming through the dirt.

"Josef, do you see the light coming through that crack?" I asked.

"Yeah, that must be a way out. I wonder where it leads to," Josef replied.

"If the opening ends up being inside the camp, we can try to escape by climbing over the fence. If the opening ends up leading to somewhere outside of the camp, we have an even better chance of escaping," I added.

"How are we going to dig our way out without getting noticed? The openings of the shafts are much too small for us to fit through," Josef asked.

"We have to figure out a way to widen the openings without any of the guards noticing. What we need is extra sticks of dynamite to blast through the shaft," I replied.

"That is a great idea, so tomorrow when we come to work do something to divert the other workers so that I can steal some sticks of dynamite," Josef said.

"Okay, I'll think of something to do that will get their attention," I replied.

The next morning, we reported to work, and right before we entered the mine I pretended to get very sick.

"Hey, what's the matter with you?" one of the guards asked.

"I don't know. All of a sudden I am having severe stomach pains," I answered while dropping to the ground, holding my stomach.

I began to moan and cough and create a scene. The prisoners and guards stopped what they were doing and stood around looking at me.

"You are just trying to get out of work. I know this trick," the guard said.

"No, I swear I am not faking it. I am having severe pain in my stomach," I responded.

"Well, then, maybe you need a trip to the hole to make you feel better," the guard replied.

The hole was an underground box that they would put prisoners in as punishment. "Please, just give me some water. I must be dehydrated," I begged.

"All right, but if you can't work you are going to the hole, the guard answered while getting me some water.

After I drank my water, I told the guard I was feeling much better and went inside the mine to find Josef.

"Were you able to get the dynamite?" I asked.

ILONA REINITZER

"Yes, I managed to get a few sticks," Josef replied as he pulled the sticks out of his pants to show me.

"Great, we need to get it in place so that we can detonate it at the same time as the civilian workers and no one hears it," I said.

There were civilian workers who were hired to detonate the dynamite in the mines and we could hear their warning right before they set off any explosives. We set up the dynamite and continued to work until it was time for the other workers to detonate their dynamite. Luckily, no one else was in the tunnels that Josef and I were in, so we didn't have to worry about anyone telling the guards what we were up to. As soon as we heard the countdown to the blasting, we lit our sticks of dynamite. Our plan worked, and no one noticed the extra explosion. We worked all day until we had tunneled our way through the shaft far enough so that we could see the outside opening.

"Look, just a couple more inches, and we can fit our way through the shaft," Josef said.

"We are going to have to wait until tonight to escape because, otherwise, the guards are going to see us," I replied.

"Let's sneak back here after everyone is sleeping tonight. If anyone sees us out of our beds, we can just tell them we are going to use the latrine," Josef responded.

At the end of the day, we made sure that there was still a large enough pile of dirt in front of the opening of the shaft so that no one would notice it. We waited until nightfall and made our way back to the mine. It was completely dark, and we couldn't risk lighting any of the lanterns for fear of being seen. Josef and I had memorized exactly what turns to make and which tunnels to go down to find the shaft we were working in.

"I can't see a thing so stay right behind me so we don't lose each other," I told Josef.

"Put your hands on the walls so we can tell when there is an opening," he replied.

We made our way through the mine by feeling our way on the walls and counting how many turns we had to make. The good thing about this mine was that the tunnels were mostly straight and long so it wasn't too difficult to find our way.

"I think we are here. I can feel the large pile of sand we left," Josef said.

"Keep digging and let's hope we find an opening," I replied.

We removed the last of the dirt to expose the opening of the tunnel.

"We did it! I can see the opening!" Josef exclaimed.

Josef carefully peaked outside of the opening.

"What do you see?" I asked.

"We are still inside the camp, and there is a double barbwire fence in front of us," Josef replied discouraged.

"Do you see any guards around?" I asked.

"No, but there is uranium waste that is lying all over the ground," Josef replied.

"Well, at this point, we have no choice but make a run for it and try to get over the fence," I said.

We both started running to the first fence and began climbing it, but we didn't make it very far before we heard one the guards yelling at us.

ILONA REINITZER

"Stop right there or I will shoot," the guard yelled.

He then fired a warning shot in the air which brought more guards over to where we were. We were taken back to the camp and put into an underground hole for the next twenty-four hours. During the time we were in the hole, they didn't give us any food and only a cup of water. Josef was put into a different hole, so I wasn't able to speak with anyone. The hole I was in was like a coffin. It was completely dark, and there wasn't enough room to stand up in. I could just barely sit up.

After what seemed like hours, one of the guards opened up the box and gave me a small cup of water and then started to close the box again.

"Wait, how long are you going to keep me in here?" I asked.

"Shut up and don't ask any questions. You are lucky we didn't kill you," he answered and slammed the door shut.

I knew that prisoners would spend a few hours in the hole if they were slow working or did some other minor infraction but I had no idea what the punishment would be for trying to escape. I dozed off after a while, and when I awoke, I felt like I could barely breathe. The air was getting very bad inside the box. I was also very hungry and very thirsty. The guard didn't give me any food, and the small amount of water he gave me didn't help much.

I tried to think of nice memories of my youth and of Květa. I wondered what she was now doing. I thought of my twin brother and the rest of my family and wondered where they were. I also remembered the story that my father had told me about the time he met Adolf Hitler in Austria. It was during World War I when they were both in the Bavarian army. He had said that Hitler enjoyed painting and was very interested in my father's paintings. My father was an excellent painter. Hitler wanted to become a painter, but his aspirations were ruined because he failed the entrance exam of the Academy of Fine Arts in Vienna in 1907 and again in 1908. My father said he seemed bitter about this and was a very withdrawn individual. I wondered what my father would have thought if he could have seen the future and realized that I was in this horrible situation because of that lunatic.

Hours went by and the oxygen level was getting worse, and I was starting to panic. I was worried that they would let me die in the hole to set an example for other prisoners. I knew I had to try to keep calm or else I would go crazy, so I did math problems in my head to keep myself occupied and eventually I dozed off again.

I was startled awake when a guard opened the box and yelled for me to get out. I later found out that I had been in the box for about twenty-four hours. I saw Josef a few meters away being taken out of another hole. We were taken back to the barracks where we saw all the rest of the prisoners standing outside in the cold without coats or shoes on (it was now October).

The guards told everyone that they had to be punished because Josef and I had attempted to escape. We all had to stand outside for about four hours before they let us go back to the barracks to go to bed.

Some of the prisoners were mad at us because of their punishment, but the majority of them said they would have attempted an escape if they had found a way out. Punishment was just a way of life at the camp and everyone got used to it. The key was to survive in order to get out one day.

ILONA REINITZER

The very next morning, Josef and I were brought before the highest officer of the camp, and we were told that we would be scheduled for another court trial within the next three months due to our attempted escape. We were also interrogated about how we managed to get the dynamite to blow up the unused shaft. Once they found out how easy it was for us to steal the sticks of dynamite, they made sure that it was now guarded at all times.

Josef and I didn't let this failed escape attempt discourage us and immediately started thinking of new ways to escape. We felt that we just needed more time to find another way out of the camp. A few weeks later, while I was down in the mine shaft, the uranium transport cart hit me in the chest, and I had trouble breathing. I was taken to the camp doctor who happened to also be a political prisoner.

"Lie down on the table and let me check your breathing," the doctor ordered.

"My name is Dr. Hovel," he added.

"I'm Julius Reinitzer," I told him.

He examined me and asked me a few questions.

"You will be all right after a day or two of rest. I think you have a slight pulmonary contusion which is what is causing your breathing difficulties," Dr. Hovel said.

"That is good news," I replied, knowing that if I had a severe injury, I would most likely die from it since they did not transfer prisoners to a real hospital.

"I will tell the guards that you need to stay here at the medical building for the next four days. If I send you back to the barracks, they will just put you back to work immediately," he added.

"What are you convicted of?" I asked him.

"I belonged to a group of doctors that were against the communists. We felt that they were interfering with our medical treatment of patients. They wanted us to give the government officials the best treatment and give substandard treatment to everyone else. Eventually, they found out that we were against them, and now here I am," he answered.

"How long are you sentenced here for?" I asked.

"Five years. How about you?" he asked.

"Fourteen years," I answered.

"You will never survive working here that long. From what I have seen, the longest anyone has ever made it is two years," he said.

"I know, that is why I am going to try and escape again," I replied.

"What is your plan?" he asked.

"I don't know yet, but once I figure it out, do you want to come with me?" I asked.

"No, I only have two more years left here, so I don't want to take the chance. I want to go back to my family and go back to practicing medicine, and if I am caught escaping then they will never let me out," he replied.

"I guess I don't blame you especially since you have it much better than the rest of us prisoners and don't have to work in the mines," I said.

"I will help you in any way that I can, though, once you come up with your plan," he offered.

"Thanks so much. I need all the help I can get to make it out of here," I replied.

Dr. Hovel showed me to a small room with two cots in it where I would be staying for the next four days. The medical building consisted of an exam room, the patient's room (where I was staying), and a small pharmacy room.

I spent the next four days recuperating, and just like the doctor had predicted, I was fine after a couple of days. While I was staying at the medical building, I noticed that it was very close to the fence surrounding the camp. The pharmacy room was the closest to the fence and was just a few meters away.

After thinking about it for a while, I came up with a plan to dig a tunnel from the floor of the pharmacy to the other side of the fence. All the buildings in the camp had dirt floors so that would make it easy. I told Dr. Hovel about the plan, and he agreed to help me.

The next day, I returned to work and told Josef of my plan. We recruited about ten other men that we trusted to help us with our plan. We knew that the more men we got involved, the riskier the escape was, but we needed several men to pull this off. We estimated that the tunnel would be done after about three weeks of digging. We had to work fast and get the tunnel completed before the ground froze for the winter.

Each day a different man would complain of an injury or illness and ask to be taken to the medical building. There Dr. Hovel would let the man into the pharmacy where he would dig through the dirt floor. We used some of the medical tools and pans to dig. We were very lucky because the ground was mainly sandy and didn't have many rocks, so it was easy to dig through. The only problem was getting rid of the dirt. We had to leave the medical building with one of the guards, and they couldn't see us carrying anything with us. We solved the problem by stuffing our pants into our boots and then filling our pants up with dirt. Then we asked to go to the outhouse where we could get rid of the dirt.

Finally, the day arrived when we finished digging through the tunnel. We all waited until the last working shift was over so that all ten of us could escape together. At 10:00 p.m., we met at the pharmacy and one by one, we crawled through the tunnel. We had made it to the other side of the fence, however, when we came out of the hole, there were guards waiting for us with guns pointing at our heads. Someone had told the guards on us. I had known it was risky to trust so many men, but it was the only way we could rotate going to the doctor without having the guards get suspicious. One of the men had told someone who gave the information to the guards for some kind of favor or better treatment.

We were all taken back to the camp and interrogated about how we were able to dig the tunnel without being noticed. We all endured hours of torture. We did cover for Dr. Hovel so that the guards didn't think he had anything to do with our attempted escape.

After a few days of our interrogation, everyone was told that they would be going back to court to have their sentences lengthened. Since Josef and I had attempted to escape twice, we were transferred to another camp near Prague to await our trial. This camp was called Fierlinger and was considered a maximum security camp. Fierlinger was a coal mine located north of Kladno, Czechoslovakia.

ILONA REINITZER

CHAPTER 17

I T WAS NOW 1952, and the communists had to continue building new concentration camps to house all the political prisoners that were being convicted on a daily basis. Prisoners at Fierlinger worked in two shifts. The first shift began at 6:00 a.m. and ended at 2:00 p.m. and the second shift began at 2:00 p.m. and ended at 10:00 p.m. At the end of each week, the prisoners had to switch shifts. Josef and I were assigned to the same shift cycle but were working in different locations in the coal mine.

Unlike the uranium mine, the inside of the coal mine was very hot. We had to drink large amounts of water to stay hydrated, but we were usually not given enough. We also took off all of our clothes and worked only in our underwear in order to stay cooler. All prisoners were given quotas on how much coal they had to mine each day and if the quotas were not met, the prisoner was not given any food. The policy was "No Work, No Food."

Many of the prisoners were unable to meet their quotas because they were too weak from dehydration. Josef and I knew that we had been sent to this camp because it was really a death camp. Most of the prisoners who worked here would die after a few months and then be replaced with new prisoners.

I immediately began to think about the plans for my next escape attempt. After a few weeks, Josef and I managed to work in the same shaft so we could talk about different escape plans.

"How are you doing?" I asked.

"Well, I'm not dead yet, but if I don't make it out of here before midsummer I will be," he replied.

"Yeah, I didn't think anything could be worse than the uranium mines, but I guess I was wrong," I said.

"I don't know how we will live through the heat of the summer in those mines. We need to get out of here soon. Have you thought of any ideas on how we can escape?" Josef asked.

"I noticed that the lighting between the guard towers has not been installed yet on the back side of the camp. Our best bet is to try to get out at night and jump the fence before they get the lights installed," I replied.

"How are we going to get over the double barbwire fence, though?"

"I haven't figured that out yet. Let's try to get over to that part of the camp and see if we can come up with something."

For the next few days, Josef and I took into consideration every building and location of the camp that would be best suited for a successful escape. Fierlinger was still in the process of being constructed, and we noticed that the double barbwire fence was completed but not all the buildings were done yet. The following week, we were able to work together again by ourselves so we discussed our escape plan.

"I overheard one of the guards saying that the lights between all the guard towers would be completed by the end of the week. We have to make our escape before then, or it will be too late and we will never get out of here," Josef stated.

"Did you notice that the small wooden barn where we get our coffee at the end of the day is only about 1.5 meters from the fence?" I asked. The barn was used to distribute coffee to the prisoners as they left the coal mine and returned to their cells at the end of each shift.

"You're right, and there aren't any lights installed at that part of the camp either. Do you think we can get over the fence without anyone seeing us?" Josef asked.

"I think we have a good chance if we make sure we are the very last ones in line because the guards will be at the front of the line and won't see us in the dark," I replied.

"What about the double barbwire? Do you think we can make it over the fence without getting stuck or cut up?"

"There is a steep hill on the other side of the fence next to the barn. If we jump off the roof of the barn, we should be able to land on the other side of the fence since the barn is so close to the fence."

"Let's hope that works. It's a good thing we are on the late shift this week. When do you want to try escaping?" Josef asked.

"Let's go tomorrow night because we can't wait any longer. Once the lights are installed, the guards will see us jumping over the fence."

The next evening, we waited until our shift ended at 10:00 p.m. and made sure that we would be the last two men in the coffee line. The guards would stay at with the front of the line heading back toward the cells so they wouldn't immediately notice that we were missing. As we hung around at the end of the line, we noticed that there were two other men waiting outside the barn, and they were not going in to get their coffee.

"Why aren't those two guys getting their coffee?" I asked.

"I don't know. It's like they are purposely standing around waiting to see if we move forward," Josef replied anxiously.

"If they don't get moving soon, they are going to blow our chances of escaping tonight," I replied uneasily.

"Do you think they know we are attempting to escape and are working for the guards?" Josef asked.

"I doubt it. You haven't told anyone about our plan, right?" I asked.

"Of course not!" Josef exclaimed.

"No one could have overheard us in the mine shaft and that was the only place we spoke about our plans. Maybe they are just trying to get some fresh air after being in the mines all day."

By now, the four of us were the only ones left who hadn't gotten our coffee, and there was a noticeable gap between us and the rest of the prisoners.

"Hey, back there. What the hell are you men waiting for?" one of the guards yelled at us.

"I guess they aren't interested in getting any coffee tonight," the other guard said.

"Yeah, maybe they enjoy the warm piss water from the mines better," the first guard laughed.

The four of us immediately ran into the barn to get our coffee and caught up with the rest of the line before the guards decided that we didn't need to get any coffee that night.

ILONA REINITZER

I couldn't risk speaking to Josef that night about our next plan of action for fear that we would be overheard. I decided to wait until we were alone again in the mines.

The next day as we were walking back to the mines, we saw workers installing the lights and knew that this would be our last chance to attempt to escape without being seen. We had to attempt to leave this evening no matter what happened or else we would end up dying at this camp anyway.

For some reason, Josef was assigned to a different area in the mine that day, so I wasn't able to speak with him at all during our shift. I was beginning to get nervous because everything seemed to be going wrong with our escape plan, and we were running out of time.

I made sure to be the last one out of the mine at the end of the shift and saw that Josef was there waiting for me. He managed to avoid being at the front of the line by telling the guard that he had to use the latrine.

It was May 21, 1952, when we tried our escape attempt for the second time. We stashed away as much food as we could hide in our pockets so that we would have something to hold us over for a few days and met back up at the coffee barn at 10:00 p.m. that evening. As we approached the barn, we saw that the same two men were standing outside the barn again. We waited hoping that they would go inside so we could be the last men in line, but they kept lingering outside looking at us. Josef and I were getting nervous because we saw that almost all the men had already gone inside for their coffee, and we needed to escape now. I decided to find out why they were taking so long again and see if I could get them to go ahead.

"Hey, don't you guys want to get your coffee tonight?" I asked.

"We don't want to risk having the guards yell at us again tonight," Josef added.

"Why don't you two go right on in and don't worry about us," one of the men replied. I later found out his name was Pavel.

The last prisoner entered the barn, and the four of us were standing there staring at each other. At this point, I decided it was now or never and I had to tell these men what our plans were so they would get into the barn.

"Listen, my friend and I are trying to get onto the roof to jump over the fence, and we need you to go through the coffee line before us and stop holding up the line," I implored.

"We were planning on doing the exact thing," Pavel said.

"What the hell are we going to do now? If all four of us escape, the guards are going to notice that a lot faster than if just two of us go," Josef replied completely stressed.

"There is no way we can try again tomorrow because once one person escapes, they will put twice as many guards over here tomorrow," Lukas answered.

"I guess we have no choice but for all of us to go together, though, it will be a lot riskier with the four of us escaping," I replied.

"All right, let's go for it. My name is Josef, and this is Julius," Josef said.

I'm Pavel, and this is Lukas," Pavel replied.

As soon as there was no one left in the barn, we jumped onto the large metal drum that held the coffee and pulled ourselves up onto the barn roof through the window. I helped each of them from below and then they grabbed my hand and pulled me up onto the roof. Then, one by one, we jumped over the portion of the fence closest to the roof. Josef, Pavel, and Lukas made it over the fence with no problem. I was the last one to jump, but my ankle got caught on the barbed wire on the top of the fence. I was hanging upside down by my ankle on the side of the fence outside of the camp. Josef, Pavel, and Lukas were already running away as fast as they could and didn't notice that I wasn't behind them. I grabbed the barbwire with my hands and finally managed to free my ankle. I fell onto the grass and ran as fast as I could to catch up with the other guys. They stopped at the top of the hill where the forest started and where they were hidden from view by anyone at the camp. Our plan had worked! None of the guards saw us because it was too dark and the lighting on that section of the camp wasn't working yet.

"Are you all right? Did you hurt your foot?" Josef asked.

"My ankle got caught in the barbwire but its fine. Let's get the hell out of here," I replied as I started running away from the camp.

We headed west toward the town of Libušín, which was only about ten kilometers away. There was a train station located in the outskirts of Libušín, which was called Mrákavy. I knew this area very well because my family had lived in Libušín when I was a child and I knew that trains leaving from this station traveled into Germany. The train station was located in the middle of a forest, so we could travel there without being seen. To our luck, we did not see or hear any police or guards the entire way.

We arrived at Mrákavy about two hours later. Normally, it wouldn't have taken us that long to get there, but we had to stay off the roads, and it was slow moving through the forest.

"Look, there are police everywhere. They are surrounding all the trains," Lukas stated as we approached the train station.

"They must have been alerted by the Fierlinger guards that we escaped," Pavel said.

"Julius, how is your ankle doing?" Josef asked.

"I can barely walk," I replied. "You need to go on without me," I continued.

"You can make it. You just need to get on the train, and I can help you aboard," Josef said.

"You are going to have to continue on and find another way to cross the border because there is no way you can make it on this train," I replied.

"We can't leave you behind. If they capture you again, they will kill you this time for sure!" Josef exclaimed.

"I'm telling you that I just can't walk anymore, let alone run. My ankle is swollen twice its normal size," I said.

"We are going to have to decide quickly on what we are going to do because the police will start searching the forest for us soon," Lukas said.

"Look, there are some bikes over there. We can take them and travel faster using the bikes," Pavel said. There was a bike stand on the side of the building that held the bikes of many of the train station employees. Since it was nighttime, they had a good chance of sneaking over to them and stealing them.

"Go on, take the bikes and head toward the German border. I will stay here and surrender," I said.

"I will tell the police that you headed toward Prague to go home," I added.

"I'm sorry, Julius. I don't want to leave you here," Josef sadly replied.

"Josef, let's go or Pavel and I have to go without you," Lukas said.

"Go quickly, the police are everywhere," I urged.

Lukas, Pavel, and Josef ran over to the bikes and started peddling down the path leading through the forest and away from the train station. Josef turned his head and looked back at me one last time and waved good-bye. I would never see him again.

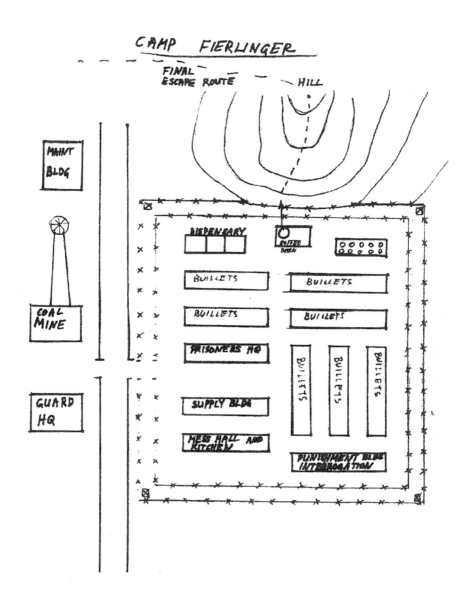

Sketch of Camp Fierlinger

CHAPTER 18

I LOOKED AROUND AND noticed a small house a few hundred meters from the train station located by the railway tracks. I dragged myself to the house and planned on surrendering to whoever was inside. I saw a young woman inside who looked like she was about twenty years old. She had a small build, had wavy brown hair, and very striking green eyes.

I crawled up to the door and opened it. I lay on the floor exhausted, dirty, and bleeding from my ankle. My clothes were ripped and falling off me because I had lost so much weight while I was a prisoner. The woman was startled by my appearance and immediately grabbed the phone.

"Please, don't be afraid. My name is Julius Reinitzer, and I just escaped from Fierlinger. I hurt my ankle, and I can't run anymore. You can call the police so I can surrender," I sighed.

"What did you do?" she asked.

"I am a political prisoner," I replied.

She looked at me and then laid the phone back down.

"So in other words, you didn't do anything. My name is Izabela. I will help you hide."

"Why are you helping me? You know that the communists will throw you in jail if they find out."

"I will tell you later, but now we have to get you out of here before someone sees you." She opened up her lunch pail and gave me her sandwich and a cup of coffee.

"Take the food and hide behind the house in the forest," she said.

"I will get off duty in about one hour and come and get you," she added.

Izabela's job was to direct train traffic on the railways by moving certain switches. I crawled out to the back of the house and hid in the forest until Izabela came and got me. She helped me hobble through the forest until we got to her house where she lived with her mother, Marta. Izabela looked exactly like her mother except that Marta looked very worn and sad. I could tell that the last several years had been a hardship for her.

"Mama, I'm home," Izabela yelled as we walked in the door.

"Come quickly and help me with this young man," she added.

"Who is he?" Marta asked.

"His name is Julius, and he is an escaped political prisoner from Fierlinger," Izabela answered.

"Why did you bring him here?" Marta asked. "The police will be searching everywhere for him, and if we get caught helping him, we will end up at Fierlinger," she added.

"I just couldn't turn him in. You know, they will send him right back there and execute him just like they did with Vaslov," Izabela said.

"I already lost one son, and I can't lose my last child," Marta stated.

"We can hide him in the chicken coop, and they will never look there if they search our house," Izabela replied. "I'm not going to help the government kill any more innocent citizens," she added.

"Come over here, Julius, and take off your filthy clothes," Izabela ordered.

"We can give him some of Vaslov's clothes. I will go get them," Marta added.

Izabela helped me wash up (I was still black from the coal mine), and they cleaned and bandaged the wound on my ankle.

"Your ankle is very swollen. You won't be able to walk on it for at least a week," Izabela stated.

"You are risking your own life if you keep me here because if any of your neighbors see me, they will tell the prison officials that you are hiding me," I replied.

"Well, don't worry about that because none of our neighbors can see into our farm. We are too far away. Anyways, they hate the government too," she added.

"Mama, please go and fix up a bed for Julius in the chicken coop, and I will heat up some soup for him," Izabela added.

Marta made up a bed for me in the chicken coop, which was located in the back of their property on the edge of the forest.

"I better get into the chicken coop now because the police will be everywhere very soon," I stated.

"I will bring you there after you finish your soup. You look like you are starving, and you aren't going to heal if you don't eat something," Izabela replied.

"Thank you for helping me. I would be a dead man if you didn't," I said wearily.

After I had eaten, Izabela and Marta helped me get inside the chicken coop. It was actually pretty large, and there was a bed made up on the floor in the very back which was hidden from the front entrance. It looked like this part of the coop was used to store food, so it was even clean. I had been expecting a small and dirty coop.

"Get some rest, and I will check on you first thing in the morning. Remember, no matter what you hear outside, do not come out of the coop," she warned.

I was so exhausted and in pain that I immediately passed out and did not wake up until I heard her voice the next day.

"Julius, wake up," Izabela said. "You have been asleep for about fifteen hours now," she added.

"I am still so tired," I replied.

"I have been checking on you all morning, but it is late in the afternoon now, and I have to go to work," Izabela said. "Here are some soup and potatoes to eat and a jug of coffee to tide you over until I return," she added.

"What time is it?" I asked.

"It's almost 5:00 p.m., and I will come back when I get off work at 1:00 a.m.," she answered.

"Thank you, Izabela," I replied.

"Did you hear anything yet regarding our escape?" I asked.

"No, but I haven't left the house at all today. I will know more once I go to work."

"Be careful and don't tell anyone. Not even your closest friends."

"I won't, even though I know that no one would ever tell the police."

"People always talk if they are being interrogated."

"You're probably right. I wouldn't say anything anyway. I need to go now. I will check in on you as soon as I return from work. Here are some bandages so you can change your dressing."

Izabela gave me a bucket of clean water and some clean bandages and then left. The first thing I did was eat the soup and potatoes because I was starving again.

After I was done eating, I stood up to relieve myself but fell over the minute I tried to put weight on my foot. I ended up hopping over to the other side of the chicken coop to relieve myself in some hay and then hopped back over to my makeshift bed. My ankle was killing me, but I knew I had to clean out my wound to prevent an infection. The cuts from the barbwire were jagged and deep. My hands were also cut from when I freed my ankle, but they weren't that bad. I spent the next thirty minutes cleaning the wound and wrapping my ankle with new bandages. I didn't feel well so after that I lay back down and ended up drifting back to sleep for a few more hours.

I woke up when I heard loud voices coming from the dirt road in the front of the house. I couldn't make out what was being said but it sounded like several men. I heard them speaking with Marta and then I heard them moving around the house and the property. I knew it was the police and was sure they were going to find me in the chicken coop. After about twenty minutes, it was quiet again.

I lay very still for the next several hours. Luckily, the chicken coop was very large and had a small loft that stored hay, which is where I stayed. I wanted to get up and get some circulation going in my legs but decided that I needed to stay lying down even though there was plenty of room to sit up. I didn't want to make a sound for fear that someone would hear me and notify the police. After what seemed like an eternity, Izabela finally came back.

"How are you doing?" she asked.

"Well, my ankle hurts a lot, and I am dying to go to the bathroom but was afraid to get up. I heard voices of several men at your house today. Did the police come?" I asked.

"Yes, my mother said that they were checking the area for escaped prisoners. They looked inside our house and around the yard but didn't notice anything suspicious so they left," she said.

"I knew they wouldn't bother to check the chicken coop. Come on, let me help you get up so you can go to the bathroom and have something to eat," she added.

Izabela helped me into their house and tended to my wound while Marta made me some pancakes with homemade jelly on them. She also fried up some eggs and gave me milk and coffee.

"I'm sorry that we don't have much real food to give you," Marta said. "After the war, the communists have made it so we can't get much meat. We live mainly off our small farm," she added.

"This is the best food that I have eaten in years!" I exclaimed.

"The food at Fierlinger was horrible, and they didn't give us much either. They only gave us bread and potatoes mixed with this horrible broth. I saw many men die of starvation there. Only young, strong men survived, and even those would eventually die from exhaustion, disease, or get executed," I added.

"We know," Izabela replied. "My brother, Vaslov, was sent there last year and was executed for helping people escape into Germany. He worked as a train conductor at Mrákavy and hid people on the train, so they could make it across the border into Germany. You are lucky that the communists didn't kill you there," she added.

"I'm sorry to hear about your brother. The only reason they kept me alive is because I was able to work in the coal mines. The minute I became sick or injured, they would have executed me," I replied.

"Vaslov was injured during the war, so he limped when he walked. He wasn't very strong so they must have decided he wasn't worth keeping alive," Marta said.

"I am very thankful that you are helping me. Without your help, I know that I would have been executed within a month. They wouldn't have even bothered sending me to their 'Kangaroo' courts and would have just killed me," I said.

"Vaslov would have wanted me to help you because he hated the communists. We had a nice life before the war and before the communists took over. He had always dreamed of leaving Czechoslovakia and traveling the world. I wish he could have done so, but now maybe you can go in his place," Izabela said.

"My twin brother went to Australia, and if I ever make it out of Czechoslovakia, I will try and find him. I won't risk going back to Prague to see my family as long as the communists are in power," I replied.

I spent the next few hours telling Izabela and Marta all about my past life and how I ended up at Fierlinger. I found out that Izabela was only a year older than me and that her brother was only twenty-eight when he was executed. Izabela's father was a soldier in the Czech army and died during the war. Marta and Izabela did not have any other family, so they were now on their own. I could see why Marta was afraid to lose Izabela. Before the sun came up, Izabela helped me back to the chicken coop to hide in case the police returned. I fell fast asleep and didn't remember much about the next few days.

I woke up to find Izabela sitting next to me in the chicken coop, looking very concerned.

"Thank goodness you are finally awake," she said.

"How long have I been sleeping?" I asked.

"You have been unconscious for the last two days," she replied.

"You had a fever, and your wound became infected. I thought you might die, but I couldn't get the town doctor or ask for medicine for you. I put some herbs on your wound from our garden that my mother said would help with the infection, and she was right. I also bathed it in salt water, which really seemed to help. The wound is much better now than it was two days ago," she added.

"Now I owe you for saving my life again," I said.

"Don't worry about that. Here, you need to eat something so you can regain your strength."

"Have you heard anything in town about our escape?" I asked.

"Yes, I'm afraid that I have bad news," she replied sadly. "I heard that they captured three of the four escaped prisoners from Fierlinger and that they are still searching for you," she added.

"I need to leave here immediately because you and Marta are going to be in danger for as long as I am here," I replied.

"You can't leave until your ankle is better or else they will capture you again for sure. I don't think they will come back to our farm any way because they already searched here. I'm sure they think you are much closer to the border by now," she said.

"I can't thank you enough for helping me even though it puts you and your mother in danger. I will leave as soon as I can walk normally again," I said.

I was greatly saddened to hear that Josef, Lukas, and Pavel had been captured. I knew they were back at Fierlinger or worse, had been executed. I realized now that hurting my ankle had actually saved me from being captured and was very grateful that Izabela hadn't turned me in. I had to leave as soon as possible and get out of the country. The longer I stayed here, the longer I would put Izabela and Marta in danger. Someone was bound to see me leave the chicken coop even though I only left at nighttime. It was only a matter of time. I also thought of my mother and older brother in Prague. I knew that the police would be interrogating them thinking that they knew where I was. I couldn't ever go back and get help from my family again.

CHAPTER 19

I SLEPT DURING THE day, and each night after work, Izabela would visit me, and we would spend hours, talking in the chicken coop. Izabela was very lonely living on the small farm with just her mother, and even if she did meet someone her own age at Mrákavy, they would only get to speak for a short time since they were leaving on the train. Izabela was a very kindhearted person and was always smiling eventhough I was putting her in danger. She reminded me a lot of Květa. I thought about her all the time and wondered where she was now. I wished that I could stay and help her and Marta on their farm for a while to repay them for everything they had done for me, but there was no chance of that.

One evening, almost two weeks since I first arrived, Izabela and I were talking in her house while Marta was asleep in the other room. I had been spending more evenings in the house since Izabela hadn't heard anymore about the police searching for me.

"I think I am well enough to leave now," I said.

"I don't think you should leave so soon. You won't be able to run far with your ankle," she replied.

"I have been thinking about it, and I decided to try and leave on the train. The police will have stopped looking for me here, and that will be my best bet to get to the border without having to walk for long distances," I said.

"I don't want you to leave yet. I am going to miss you and won't have anyone my age to talk to," she said.

Izabela looked at me with tears in her eyes and then leaned over and started to hug me tightly.

"I will miss you too, Izabela. I would like so much to stay and help you and your mother. I don't want to put you and Marta in anymore danger," I said.

Izabela began to kiss me. I didn't want to hurt her feelings because I knew that she liked me and was very lonely.

"Please stop, you will only make it worse for us both when I have to leave tomorrow night," I said.

"No, I don't want to stop," she replied while continuing to kiss me all over. "I don't want to live having any regrets on doing what I feel is right. Who knows what will happen tomorrow or the next day or next year. For all I know, the communists will ruin every chance for happiness that I will ever have so I want to live for today," she said.

"I have a girlfriend who I am going to try and locate again someday. This madness will end one day, and you will meet someone who you can share the rest of your life with. Even if I didn't have a girlfriend, there is no way we could ever be together. You and your mother will just end up in prison if I stay here," I said.

Izabela began to cry, and we continued to sit there together for the rest of the night until we fell asleep. The next morning Marta found us asleep in the living area and quickly woke us up.

"The sun is up. You need to get back to the chicken coop," Marta said. "You are putting us all in danger," she added.

I jumped up and quickly made my way back to the chicken coop. I knew that I had to leave that evening when the sun went down. My ankle was much better, and I could walk on it again. Izabela followed me to the chicken coop, and I told her my plans to leave that evening.

"I already knew what you were going to say and that you were planning on leaving," Izabela said sadly.

"I have already stayed much too long," I replied.

"I know. I will prepare you a backpack with some food, water, and extra clothes that had belonged to Vaslov," she said.

"I can't thank you enough for what you have done for me," I replied.

"I just hope you make it safely out of the country. I will give you the train schedule so you will know where each train is headed and what time they leave," she added.

Izabela then left so I could go back to sleep and get some rest before I had to travel for the next few days. When the sun went down, Izabela returned and brought me back to the house. Marta had prepared dinner for me. After I ate, Izabela gave me the backpack and the train schedule.

"Izabela, I know you will meet someone and live a happy life. I will never forget the two of you," I added.

I gave them each a hug and left heading through the woods toward the train station. I looked back one more time and saw Izabela sadly standing by the door with tears in her eyes. I felt terrible, but I knew it was time for me to leave.

CHAPTER 20

I ZABELA HAD TOLD me that there was a train transporting coal to Germany that left from Mrákavy each evening. I decided that I was going to get into one of the rail cars containing coal and head toward the border. I hid in the forest until I saw the coal train pull up. It stopped so that the police could verify the transport papers and inspect the train. I watched as one of the policemen looked over the rail cars at the back of the train and when he was finished, I jumped into the last rail car that was filled with coal. I covered myself with coal and waited until the train departed.

My plan was to stay on the train until we arrived at a town called Cheb and then I would cross over the border on foot. I couldn't see from underneath the coal but I could hear the conductor state the name of each town that the train stopped in. Cheb was approximately 170 km from Libušín, but I knew that it would take several hours to get there because of all the stops and inspections that would take place.

It was sometime the next afternoon when the train came to a stop and didn't move for quite some time. I began to get nervous, wondering why we weren't continuing on. Finally, after what seemed like an eternity, I heard the conductor speaking with someone outside the train station telling them that there was a problem with the train and that it would not be going any further until it was repaired.

It was dark by now so I crawled out of rail car and started to walk west toward the German border. I soon realized that we had stopped in a town called "Žatec" which was still about seventy kilometers away from the border. I quickly walked away from the train station until I was safely hidden by an old deserted barn and then stopped to take a break and eat the food that Izabela had packed for me. I hadn't eaten since I left her house the night before. When I opened the backpack, I noticed an old, worn leather wallet in the backpack. There wasn't much money in the wallet, but I knew Izabela had put it in there to help me, and it was probably all the money she had.

After I had eaten, I continued walking until I made it to the next train station. By the time I arrived there, my ankle was hurting quite a bit, and it was causing me to limp again. Over the past two weeks, I hadn't walked very much and, therefore, didn't realize that my ankle wasn't fully healed. I was so glad that Izabela had given me the money because I knew I wouldn't be able to walk to the border anymore and needed to take the train.

I tried to buy a train ticket to Cheb but realized that I didn't have enough money. I didn't have enough money for any ticket as Izabela had only given me twenty koruna and the cheapest ticket was thirty-five koruna. I stood around the train station for a while trying to decide what to do next. My ankle was just hurting too much for me to walk anywhere. I noticed a young girl around eighteen years old who was watching me, so I decided to approach her and see if she would help me.

"Hello, my name is Karl. What's yours?" I asked as I lied about my name.

ILONA REINITZER

"It's Lenka," she replied.

"Where are you traveling to?" I asked.

"Oh, I am not taking a train. I work here in the office," she said.

"Is your shift over now? I was hoping that you might like to keep me company until my train leaves," I asked.

I was hoping to get friendly enough with this girl so that she might help me. I had run out of any other ideas and she seemed very friendly.

"Okay, I guess I could hang out for a little while," she answered.

"So how long have you worked here?" I asked, making more small talk.

"Only six months since I finished school. I haven't seen you before. Where are you from?" she asked.

"I just graduated from Karls University in Prague, and I am heading to Cheb for a job interview."

"I was watching you because I was trying to figure out why you are limping and covered with black soot."

I realized that I was still covered in black soot from hiding in the coal compartment so I made up a quick story.

"I was running late while trying to catch my train out of Prague, so I took a short cut through the train yard. I tripped on something and fell into a pile of coal and twisted my ankle."

"That's awful. Did you at least make your train?"

"Yes, but it wasn't worth it because now I am filthy and my ankle really hurts."

"Why don't we go inside where you can sit down, and I will find some ice to put on your ankle."

"Good idea. Can I buy you a cup of coffee?"

"Sure, let me go get it though so you don't have to limp over there."

I started to search my coat pocket, pretending to look for my wallet.

"I can't find my wallet. It had all my money and my ticket in it."

"Let's go back outside and see if we can find it. Maybe you dropped it somewhere."

We searched for about thirty minutes when I finally pretended to give up.

"I don't know what I will do now. I can't walk, and I don't have money or my train ticket."

"I wish that I could give you a train ticket, but I don't have access to them from my office. All I have is twenty korunas, and that won't buy you a ticket."

"Let me check my backpack. I think I had twenty korunas stashed away in there for emergencies."

I rummaged through my backpack and then pulled out the twenty korunas from Izabela.

"Sure enough, here it is. If you will lend me your twenty korunas, and I add it to my twenty korunas, I will be able to buy a train ticket."

"You can have my twenty korunas, but the only ticket you will be able to buy is for Mrákavy."

"I have an aunt who lives in Mrákavy, so I can go to her, and she will be able to give me the money that I need to get to Cheb."

Lenka gave me her money, and I bought a ticket going back to Mrákavy. I had no other choice, and since I couldn't walk, I just wanted to go somewhere where I could rest, so I planned on returning to Izabela's house. Lenka kept me company until my train left, and I thanked her again for giving me the money. I hated having to lie to her, but it was just too risky telling her the truth. I waved good-bye from my train window and then headed toward the bathroom to wash off the black soot. I spent the majority of the train ride hiding in the bathroom so I wouldn't be noticed.

I got off the train in Mrákavy, and no one seemed to notice me. I made my way back to Izabela and Marta's house. I didn't know what else to do and figured I would hide in the chicken coop for one more night until I came up with a new plan. It was still dark, so I quietly knocked on their back door. Marta opened the door and looked shocked.

"Julius, what are you doing back here?" she asked.

"Quickly, come inside," she added before I could reply.

I told her the story about what had happened in the past twenty-four hours.

"I'm sorry to bother you again, but I didn't know what else to do," I said.

"Izabela is working a double shift so she won't be returning until tomorrow morning. You can hide in the chicken coop again tonight, but you need to promise me that you won't let Izabela know that you are back," Marta said. "She is devastated that you left, and I don't want her to get her hopes up that you are coming back to stay," she added.

"I promise that I will leave as soon as the sun goes down tomorrow, and I won't let Izabela know I am back," I assured Marta. I knew that

Marta was very frightened and worried about getting in trouble with the government.

"I will make you a sandwich to eat before you go back to the chicken coop," Marta said.

"Thank you. I already ate everything that Izabela gave me to take with me," I told her.

"Take your clothes off, and I will get you some other old clothes from Vaslov. If you walk around covered in coal, you are going to look suspicious," she added.

Marta gave me a new set of clothes to put on and then made my sandwich. When I finished eating, I went back to the chicken coop that still had my makeshift bed in it. I was wondering why Izabela hadn't cleaned it up yet. Maybe she wanted to keep it there a few more days to remember me by. I slept the day away until Marta woke me up in the late afternoon.

"I brought you some money and two train tickets," she said. "This ticket will take you Prague and then you need to switch trains to go to Pilsen. You need to switch directions so that you aren't seen in this area again," she added.

"I don't want to take any more money from you," I replied. "I would if I could repay you and send you money once I get out of the country but I know that it will only get you in trouble with the government if they find out that you helped me," I added.

"Don't think twice about it. Vaslov would have wanted us to help you and I want you to go and see the world for him," she replied. "I've already bought the train tickets so you need to take them," she added.

ILONA REINITZER

"Thank you so much for everything you and Izabela have done for me," I replied.

"Here is some food to take with you, but you must go tonight," she said.

I gave her a hug, thanked her again, and told her that I would not return. When the sun set, I left the chicken coop and headed back to Mrákavy.

CHAPTER 21

I GOT ON THE train at Mrákavy which took me to the suburb of Prague. I got off at the Smichov station and switched trains heading toward Pilsen. This train was a commuter train which stopped at every small town. When we arrived at the Radotin station, I noticed that the SNB (Communist National Security Corps) police boarded the train and began checking personal identification cards, starting at the front of the train. I made my way to the back of the train knowing that my railcar would be the last one checked. The train departed with the police onboard.

The next station was in Dobřichovice. I knew this region very well because my brother, Jan, and I used to camp in this area on weekends when we were teenagers. I knew every town, river, and bridge in the area. The railway followed along a river called "Berounka" and the train would cross a bridge over this river right after the next stop in Dobřichovice.

The train stopped in Dobřichovice, and I kept watching which railcar the police were in. They were getting close to the railcar I was in, so I knew I had to jump out of the train before they found me. I knew that the water in the Berounka River was deep enough that I could jump into it from the train when it crossed over the bridge. The police were in the railcar right before mine when the train crossed over the bridge. I opened up the window and jumped into the river. As I swam to the shore, I saw the lights from the train disappearing into the darkness.

I was cold from the water but since it was summertime, I warmed up quickly as I began to walk in the hilly terrain near the river. I began looking for a place to hide before the sun came up. I noticed several deer tracks, so I followed them until I got to a small river. I spent the rest of the night, sleeping out in the open. It was actually somewhat comfortable sleeping outside in the open air on some moss compared to being im the chicken coop.

The next morning, I laid out my clothes and money in the sun to dry and looked around for something to eat. I found some mushrooms and berries to eat for breakfast. When my clothes were dry, I began walking west again toward the German border. I stayed out of the towns and away from roads and stuck to the hilly grasslands. I spent the next evening, sleeping in the forest. I was lucky that the weather was nice, and it never did rain on me.

I couldn't find anything to eat the next morning and was very hungry by the afternoon, so I decided to use some of my money to get some food at a small restaurant on top of one of the hills. This was a restaurant used mainly by farmers, hikers, and local villagers, so I thought it would be safe. I sat down at a table and ordered some food. As I was waiting for my food, I listened to the conversation the waiter was having with one of the other guests. The waiter told him how much he hated the communist government because they had taken away his restaurant back in 1948. It had been in his family for generations, but now it belonged to the government. After I had eaten, I left and went into the nearby forest to find a place to stay overnight.

I kept thinking about what the waiter had said and decided that I was going to go back to the restaurant and see if this man might help me. I knew that it was still a long way to the border, and my ankle was still hurting. I waited until the restaurant opened and went in and sat down. There were no other guests there at the time since it was so early. The same waiter greeted me and then sat down to talk.

"Hello, my name is Yanko. I noticed you here yesterday, but you aren't from this area, are you?" Yanko asked.

"No, I'm just passing through and doing some hiking," I replied.

"Well, let me warn you that this isn't a good area for hiking," he said. "You need to be careful because there are resistance groups in the surrounding hills," he added.

"Have you seen any police nearby?" I asked.

"Not in the past few days, but they are constantly coming by and asking me if I have seen any suspicious-looking men," he said.

"I hear gunfire on a regular basis, so I can only assume they are fighting with these groups. Are you with the resistance?" he asked.

I hesitated because I felt I could trust him, but yet I still wasn't certain.

"You look like you need help. You can trust me because I hate the communists," Yanko said.

I decided to tell him my story because I was desperate for help to get to the border. If I kept going along on foot I would probably run into the police. He told me that he would help anyone he could to fight the communist government.

"Come back tonight, and I will leave you my bicycle along with some food, maps, and a compass," he said. "I will leave it by the back door," he added.

I thanked him and left after eating breakfast which Yanko told me "was on the house" for all noncommunist Czech citizens. I spent the day, sleeping in the nearby forest so I would have energy to travel all night. When it was dark, I went back to the restaurant and sure enough, there was a bicycle and backpack waiting for me. I circled the restaurant a few times to see if there was any police or soldiers inside, but I did not see any. I waited for about an hour and finally felt it was safe enough to me to run up and get the bike and backpack. Yanko turned out to be trustworthy after all. I rode the bicycle all night, using the map that Yanko had left for me. I headed west and stayed on the back roads as much as possible.

In the morning, I came to the town of Nýrsko. I passed by one of the safe houses that I had established two years ago and debated whether or not I should stop and ask for help getting across the border. I decided against it because I did not know what had changed in the last two years while I was in the concentration camps. This might not even be a safe house anymore. It was just too risky. I was going to attempt to get across the border on my own.

I spent the rest of the day hiding in a nearby cemetery, which was about eight kilometers away from the German border. I planned to go through the forest as much as possible for the remaining way to the border, so I hid the bicycle under leaves and branches so I could continue the rest of the way on foot.

ILONA REINITZER

I waited until it was dark outside and then crossed over a main road between Nýrsko and Všeruby which was heavily guarded. As I approached the road, I heard cars, motorcycles, voices, and dogs barking. I hid in the forest and waited for the road to clear before I ran across it. I continued heading southwest through a very dense forest. It was slow moving, but at least, I knew I wouldn't be seen.

I was navigating the direction I was traveling by using the compass that Yanko had given me, but after an hour, I sensed I was going in circles. I figured out that the compass wasn't working correctly, so I oriented myself using the stars. I found the Big Dipper, then the North Star, and used them to continue heading southwest. I knew the border had to be close by.

Finally, I saw a large opening in the forest and there was a tall guard tower about fifty meters away. I went back into the forest to find a spot on the fence to cross where the guard tower was further away but soon realized that they were everywhere along the fence. I had no choice but to make a run for it and try to scale the fence while the lights weren't shining on me.

I waited until the lights just passed me and ran toward the fence. There were rocks on both sides of the fence, which made a lot of noise when I stepped on them. I thought for sure that the guards would hear me and start shooting at me. For some reason, no one heard or saw me and I never saw any guards either. The guard in the tower must have been sleeping. It only took me a few seconds to climb the 2.5-meter high fence. I was still on the Czech side of the border and ran as fast as I could until I reached a small brook. I knew this was the border because I saw the "border stones" that were lying on each side of the brook. On the Czech side of the brook, the stones were marked with "CS," and on the German side, they were marked with "B" for Bavaria.

My luck had finally changed, and by some miracle none of the guards saw or heard me when I ran across the border. Even though I had made it into Germany, I kept on running for the next ten kilometers, limping the entire way. I wanted to make sure that no one was after me because I was determined to get out of Czechoslovakia once and for all.

The next morning, I made it to Furth im Wald and reported to the United States Military. They sent me to the US hopsital in Nürnberg where I stayed until my leg healed. The first thing I did was try to find out where Květa was. I contacted the International Red Cross again, but they did not have any record of her. I also tried to locate the military personnel that I had worked for but found out that they had all already been relocated back to the United States. I made a few new friends, and they helped me try to locate Květa, but we had no luck finding her.

I had to decide what I was going to do next. I was definitely not going back to Czechoslovakia or any other communist country, so I figured my options were to stay in Germany and find a job or join the US Army in Germany. I decided to join the army because that would enable me to finally go to the United States as I had always dreamed about. I was sent to the United States for my basic training. I first became airborne and then later joined the Special Forces (Green Berets) in 1952. I volunteered for the Korean War in February 1953 but was told that I was needed back in Germany due to my knowledge of the area and because I spoke English, German, and Czech. I served two tours of duty in the Special Forces during the Vietnam War where I used up a few more of my "nine" lives but that is another story.

EPILOGUE

J ULIUS REINITZER SPENT his army career moving back and forth between the United States and Germany. He was stationed at Bad Tölz, Germany several times during his career and also at Fort Bragg, North Carolina, and Fort Devens, Massachusetts. He continued to serve in the Special Forces military unit until he retired as a sergeant major in 1982. He joined the first Special Forces unit ever created and was the last one from this group to retire thirty years later in 1982.

Julius met a German woman named Helga Blome while he was stationed in Germany. They were married in 1956 in Garmsich, Germany, and had two daughters. His wife and her family also had a terrible time during World War II, so they had much in common.

Due to the communist rule, Julius was never allowed back into Czechoslovakia to visit his family until 1990 (after the Berlin Wall fell in 1989). A few years after the end of the communist rule in Czechoslovakia, Julius received an apolgy letter from the Czech government. Since then, he and his family have visited many times. His older brother and family still live in Prague along with his half-brother (his mother had remarried and had one son, named Viktor, who was born in 1950). Julius was not able to return to Prague to see his mother before she died in 1982 even though he lived only four hundred and forty kilometers away at the time.

Květa left England and immigrated to the United States. She contacted the International Red Cross and found out that Jan was in Sydney, Australia, at the time. She got his address, and they exchanged letters. Jan left Australia about two years later and moved to Hollywood, California, where he met Květa. Together they continued to search for Julius until they were finally notified by the International Red Cross that he had joined the US Army and were given his address.

Julius was reunited with Jan in 1960 in the United States. Jan lived in Hollywood until he died in 1989. Jan never married or had any children and had no other family in the United States except for his twin brother. Julius and Jan were able to see each other on a regular basis throughout their lives.

By the time, Julius heard from Květa he was already married, and his first daughter had just been born, so he did not reunite with Květa again. Květa later married and had children of her own. Květa's father, Cestmir, died in prison before he was due to be released. Julius was never able to find his friend Soucek.

In 1992, Julius and his older brother, Jiri, took a trip back to Libušín to see if they could locate Izabela. They went back to the farmhouse, but it had been torn down, so they went to the train station at Mrákavy. An employee at the train station did remember the family who had lived there and gave Julius and Jiri their new address in the town of Kladno. In Kladno, they found Izabela's daughter who told them that her mother was terminally ill and in the hospital. She was no longer conscious, so they decided not to go the hospital to see her. Izabela's daughter did know about the story of Julius's stay in the chicken coop from her mother, and she was happy to hear that he was alive and to hear the rest of his story. Her family had always wondered what became of him.

Julius retired in New Hampshire where he still lives with his wife. At the time of this printing, they celebrated their fifty-sixth wedding anniversary. His two adult daughters, Ilona and Elaine, and their families also live in New Hampshire. New Hampshire's state motto "Live Free or Die" couldn't be more fitting for someone who spent his life fighting for freedom.

Picture of Julius Reinitzer at the age of 21 (taken in 1949 in Prague)

Pictured from left to right: The Nanny, Julius, Jirina (mother),
Jiri, Jan (father), and Jan

CPSIA information can be obtained at www.ICGtesting.com
Printed in the USA
BVOW071659151112

305586BV00001B/2/P